Clown Gravy

stories by

Misti Rainwater-Lites

ROADSIDE PRESS

toc

And I noticed that I smelled bad.
In fact I stank.
But all my co-workers stank as well.
Nobody would notice,
& life

was the great in-between.

Joe Pachinko (1960-2017)

ACE OF CUPS

Jessie felt herself building a case against Kirk as he dripped beer sweat all over her and bit into her neck. He liked to mark her. She was his bitch. Kirk made decent money as a plumber and he had a big dick. In Kirk's alcohol hazy mind those two facts covered a multitude of sins. Wasn't it bad enough that Jessie drove them from San Antonio to South Padre, Kirk in the passenger seat guzzling Coors Light tall boys talking about the woman he divorced in 1980whatever?

"She cheated on me first. She started it in high school when she fucked Tommy Ramirez while she was wearing a promise ring I worked my ass off at Orange Julius to put on her damn finger. I was young, dumb and full of cum."

It wasn't like he knew what he was doing down there. He did not. They had been together since February, here it was July, and Kirk had not once made Jessie cum. She stayed for the usual reasons. She had nowhere else to go. And there was the matter of Kirk's big beautiful brown dick. Size had never mattered to Jessie. Ethnicity? Whatever. But here she was at the ridiculous age of forty-two crazy deep in love with a big dick native son of San Antonio. Jessie sucked Kirk's dick with tears in her eyes. She felt so Billie Holiday, so Janis Joplin. So Amy Winehouse. Love was such a losing game. She wasn't winning much with her industrious, heartfelt blow jobs. Knowing this inspired the tears.

"Where are you, babe?"

"I'm here."

"You're like a damn log. Don't you love me no more?"

"The sweat is too goddamn much. The sweat and the slobber. Lo siento. I ain't feelin' it."

"Your pussy is wet."

"My pussy is a traitor and an idiot."

Jessie felt mocked by the painting hanging on the wall. Bluebonnets. A windmill. Texas our Texas. All hail the mighty state. The only thing Texas had ever given Jessie was an accent. A North Texas accent, no less. Hollywood never got it right. Too much twang. One size fits all. "Size doesn't matter," Jessie said to her reflection in the smudged bathroom mirror as she waited for the shower to heat up. She brushed her teeth and thought Well At Least I Got Good Eyes. Kirk had never complimented her eyes but various exes had. They were mutable. Grey then green then blue.

The breakfast buffet was sad. As Jessie sipped terrible coffee she watched mindless adults and their yammering children, still in pajamas, load up on bright yellow bananas and scrambled eggs and bacon that didn't look crispy. Kirk wolfed down his bacon and eggs, oblivious to Jessie's contempt. Things were breaking. Things were falling apart. Jessie gazed at Kirk with the eyes he never complimented and willed him to do or say something endearing. Something tender. Something sweet.

"I need a drink," Kirk said.

"Bingo. Of course you do. I'm a lot to endure sober."

"Why are you such a bitch all of a sudden? We're in South Padre. You should be ecstatic. Who knows when we'll be back."

They wouldn't be back. Jessie saw herself returning to the travel trailer they called home and packing her things in Walmart bags. She had left him twice before. Once because he laughed at her when he walked in on her during a vigorous vibrator session. And then the last time during Fiesta when Kirk got drunk in a downtown bar and hit on the congenial barmaid.

"He's a loser. I don't know what you see in that man," Jessie's mother said the last time Jessie showed up at her place in Dallas with bulging Walmart and Dollar Tree bags and eyes swollen from crying. Jessie turned it into a poem, same as always. All the trash and horror of her life ended up in bleak poems that did not rhyme. Jessie thought of herself as the girl in the fairy tale spinning all that straw into gold. But Jessie often wondered if the straw remained straw. She was not convinced that she was capable of creating gold.

"You should write poems about Jesus," Travis said. Travis was Jessie's fourth stepdad but she did not see him as such. When she mentioned him on rare occasion she referred to him as her mom's fifth husband. He married her mom at a drive-up window in Las Vegas when Jessie was thirty-five. Travis loved John Wayne, Jesus and Trump equally. He met the men from his church for Bible study each Wednesday morning at Dairy Queen even though he was diabetic. The home Travis shared with Jessie's mother was decorated with bluebonnets and windmills and mounts. Ram heads. Deer heads. Jessie preferred the travel trailer. It was so minimal. No walls, really, to hang shit on.

"Do you miss me?" Jessie asked Kirk when he called. All she wanted was for him to beg her to come back, to say something she'd heard in an Air Supply song or on a "90210" episode during an especially soulful exchange between Dylan and Brenda.

"I miss your pussy. Could you just put it in a box and Fed Ex it to me?"

There had been red flags when they met in the bowling alley bar that fateful day in February...Kirk's insistence on hooking up right away, his taste in music. He fist pumped when "Paradise City" started to boom from the crackling speakers. But Jessie was adept at ignoring red flags. She saw red flags and thought, "Whee. I must be at the circus."

"Damn. She is rockin' the hell outta that bikini," Kirk said, raising his bottle of Corona in salute as he strolled along the crowded beach with Jessie. Jessie felt fat and ugly and old in her twenty dollar Faded Glory one piece. The woman in the bikini was a beer commercial. Big tits flat stomach long brown hair streaked with golden highlights. She flashed a Colgate smile at Kirk. "Get her number. Don't let her get away. Go man go," Jessie said.

"Don't be jealous, sweetheart. She is way the hell outta my league."

"Am I really the best you can do? Don't sell yourself short. You're a big dick plumber with a truck and a travel trailer. The world is pretty much your oyster."

"Fuck you."

"It takes two, as you love to say."

"I need another beer. You are ruining my vacation."

"I need cyanide. You are ruining my life."

"It would shatter my heart if I thought you were being serious."

"You won't remember any of this tomorrow."

"I hope you're right. Except for the bikini chick. I wouldn't mind remembering that."

There was a boy in San Antonio, a seven-year-old boy. Logan. Jessie's son. He lived with his dad, Jessie's second ex-husband, in a brand-new brick house in a gated subdivision. Jessie saw him on weekends. Jessie's heart was lacerated. She would never be the strong, happy, successful mother her son deserved. Jessie saw her first therapist when she was eight.

"He said there wasn't anything wrong with you. You were just a spoiled brat," Jessie's mom said with a laugh.

"Oh yeah. I was spoiled as hell. Living on Malt-O-Meal and fish sticks, wearing clothes from Goodwill and K-Mart. What kind of therapist would say that, anyway? What a piece of shit."

Jessie received a disability check each month for anxiety and depression but she wasn't on meds. She had quit Paxil cold turkey when she was twenty because she missed having orgasms. There had been a few psych ward vacations. Jessie always enjoyed the waffles and art therapy.

"Why can't you love Daddy again and live with us, Mommy?" Logan asked a few months ago, sucking on his thumb as tears streamed down his cheeks. Jessie had wanted to die. And that was one moment of many. Being a mother to a beautiful, sweet boy had been the most brutal experience of Jessie's life. So much love. Deep and wide. She had never felt more inadequate, more wretched. It killed Jessie that Logan still sucked his thumb and held onto a stuffed animal he'd had since he was a newborn. A giraffe he called Toby. God. God. God. This world. This life. All you can do is suck your thumb and hold onto something, anything. There has to be some approximation of love. Love that refuses to fucking die. Logan had his thumb and Toby. Kirk had his beer and lust. What the hell did Jessie have?

"Don't drown in the four of cups," the tarot reader told Jessie a couple of weeks ago. The reader tapped her long purple and yellow nails on the card that depicted a man sitting beneath a tree looking petulant. His arms and legs crossed. Three golden chalices on the ground before him. A hand from a cloud above his head offering him a fourth golden chalice. Nah. I'm good. I'm solid. I don't need that shit.

"Ennui. Lassitude. You feel like shit is fucked up, right? Life sucks. We get through it, somehow, then we die in some damn way. Not to be a joy killer. Just keepin' it real. The problem is you're thinkin' happiness is external. It ain't. It's an inside job."

The tarot reader's name was Rebecca. Rebecca held up the card that depicted a largen golden chalice. The chalice without malice. The chalice of all chalices. The holy fucking grail. The Ace of Cups.

"This," Rebecca said with a smile.

"This is yours, baby girl. The peace that surpasses all understanding. You are allowed to treat yourself to this."

"But...how? What can I do? I wouldn't know where the hell to begin."

"Love the fuck outta yourself. That's it. That's everything."

Daniel Johnston's plaintive voice sang in Jessie's head as she gazed at the Ace of Cups.

"How am I supposed to give love if I ain't never got love?"

Love the cookie fortune. Love the Air Supply song. Love

the subliminal suggestion. Love the stab in the dark. Love the guess. Love the jigsaw puzzle with one missing piece.

It ended in a karaoke bar. Jessie sang "My Man" by Billie Holiday. Jessie watched from the stage as Kirk headed to the bar to get another beer. Nada. It was all nada. The ache the throb the blow jobs the tears the kisses the love deep and wide. All the energy and effort and emotion added up to exactly nada.

"You did good," Kirk said as Jessie sat down at their table.

"How would you know? I mean...oh gee thanks."

"I am having the time of my life."

"Aren't we all?"

A skinny blonde in a short pink dress began singing a Selena song. Kirk hollered his drunken appreciation. "Damn, girl! You got it!"

Jessie stood up without a word and walked past the tables and cigarette machine to the door that led out into the balmy South Padre night. Miracle of miracles Jessie saw a falling star. She made a wish and hit the road back to San Antonio.

FINGERED

In the late village bare except for leaves there was fighting at night but the nights were cool and vetiver-scented. Look. Mira. We think. We read. We are not peasants thrilled with banana lotion donations and pockets of white rice. There is a class that controls a country that is stupid. They make money out of it, a veritable fuckton. The hell with that noise.

We make a brew of buds from a special cactus plant. Nightmare juice. SwooncaKe sauce. Stops time in its motherfucking tracks. Turns the world colors no one has named yet. Rivers of menstrual blood. Raging. Pulsating glittering starving vortex. Rainbowed deserts and envious forests. Spirits blackberrying dominion. Swirling energies cherrying oblivion. Deer warriors protecting hermetic glow. No one knows how to still this process, dull this shine, capture this chaos. Pero. Clocks and cages persist. Plump black grapes snatched with gnarled blistered fingers wither inside shit caked assholes. Raisins for breakfast.

Ten a.m. Drinking tequila. No money, nowhere to go, nothing. Absolute nada. Cheap acrylic paint…Apple Red, Lemon Yellow, Orlando Orange, Cotton Candy Blue…drips down cave walls. By cave of course I mean San Antonio studio apartment. Globs of paint like bubble gum all over the tacky brown carpet. Fuck the deposit. "Trout Mask Replica" spins and chocolate incense snakes to the low ceiling. The frozen cheese pizza bakes to a crisp in the oven.

This is a history of San Antonio, Texas. Across from El Alamo is a bar where a woman will let her father buy her shots of tequila and bottles of beer and will then kill him with her concealed handgun after sucking on a paleta. The road to Mexico is littered with plastic crosses and flowers. Mexicans don't forget their dead. Texans in general, tough as they are, do not forget their dead. Despite all the strip malls and shooting ranges and football games Texans are a sentimental lot. Look at me, forty-nine years old and still crying in my Shiner Bock over the ghosts of heartaches past. Steve overdosed on heroin when we were in tenth grade. Curtis got killed by a pimp outside a casino in North Las Vegas on the second night of our honeymoon. Pablo got drunk and drove his Dodge Ram into a Ross Dress For Less hours after I swallowed his cum. He killed himself and twelve other human beings. And those were just my men, not my blood kin. The Brazos River is swollen with the blood of my dead kin. I'm an orphan and the last of my line. I'm not sure if this is a tragedy. If it is, it is one of many. People die every fucking second in various ways. And so it goes. Vonnegut said so.

Last night I had another animal dream. Owls and cockroaches and rats and ponies are my familiars. What a motley crew, gabbling news I can't use as I toss and turn in sweat soaked sheets. The boy owl. I call him Oscar. He tells me, "You could go down that road as far as it would take you without ever stepping foot outside your door." Thanks. Gracias. You're the best. The woman owl. I call her Olga. She says, "A treadmill won't begin to fix your problems." Shit. Tell me something I don't already know, bitch. The cockroaches I won't even try to translate. They are legion. Filthy survivor asshole motherfuckers. The rats are the worst. Your life will end in a prison. Your life is a sinking ship. Your ship is a lollipop. Your prison is unrequited love. You will never ever ever transcend the mud of Texas you slobbering malnourished bitch. *You reek of unwashed hair and unwashed cunt. There's no reason for you to own an Android. You're an android in a sea of Victoria's Secret models and Instagram white teeth big ass celebrities. You aren't as fabulous as you think you are. You aren't even addicted to anything. What kind of loser bitch isn't addicted to anything? The worms will writhe their blasphemous ballet all over you and you will still be conscious, comparing yourself to reality stars and Latina cartoons. You have no ass to speak of. Your tits are mediocre at best. Why do you own a phone? No one requires your presence. Die bitch die. You are a waste of flesh a waste of space.*

Muchas gracias, rats, and an infinity of besos for keeping my shadow firmly attached to the heels of my feet. Who needs Wendy? Then the ponies (bless their hearts) blow some sunshine up my ass, Inspirobot style. **Annie got it right! The sun WILL in fact come out tomorrow! You can bet your bottom dollar on that shit! God wants to see you succeed! So does Jesus! So does Santa Claus! You can beat the system! All you need is one good scratch card! Rape is a thing we survive! Let's live for the day when Disney Pixar turns "I Spit On Your Grave" into a musical cartoon starring an optimistic unicorn! The prince (Chad from Calabasas) will rub the unicorn's purple glittery horn beneath**

the misty rainbow and magically transform the unicorn into a cheerleader voiced by Reese Witherspoon! Don't give up! You are in it to WIN it, cowgirl!

I hope to stay where I live, near the coconut scented abyss. The ice cream is quite satisfactory. Breathing alone until my dark is bright. The earth is mine because I walk and bleed on it. I will make it but it might take me. The Devil isn't dead, he's just playing poker in Acuna. The orchards are alive with fume. I know every speckle of my plums. These tools no fall can flake. Mediocre platitudes sustain the cud chewing masses. I have no need for tongue. I do not deal in dry desire. The Divine Absurd keeps like a parakeet in my cage. I'm a roaring girl, a kind of bonfire. Fire is my will and water is my way. I don't play favorites. I don't play for the peanut gallery. Lust wears my ass out. If I have a soul it's copper.

This rose stays. You green thing in my way. The weather's wrong. Even the loose threads are speaking. This, mijo, is a history of Bexar County, Texas. This is a package of marshmallows on a picnic table at Garner State Park. Esta es mi culo! Whoa! Technology! This is mustard. This is white bread. This is Sam's Choice Cola. This is nada. This is Hurricane Harvey. This is Fiesta Texas roller coaster. This is losing lottery ticket. This is Dodge Ram pick-up truck. This is travel trailer rusting in the Balcones Heights smug dick suck sun. This is cinnamon mouthwash. This is mint dental floss. This is blue toothbrush. This is Alcoholics Anonymous. This is Five Below Buddhism. This is Frank Zappa record, warped. It was really cool once, it really got me through. This is itchy khaki Goodwill britches. This is big deal action movie. Box office? Blow me, baby. This is silicone implants. If you wanna keep Chad you WILL go under the knife. This is San Antonio beer commercial. Nico LaHood for PRESIDENT. This is Tom Petty Eddie Money Taylor Swift Beyonce Sammy Hagar RADIO. Rawk. This is organic banana. This is coleslaw. This is second or third church wedding. Jesus wants us to enjoy our Great Value sex lives. This is Avon. This is Mary Kay. Jesus wants us to be pretty. This is Tupperware. This is Precious Moments. This is ULTA. This is booty call. This is flea market.

An all nude dancer (Koffi? Kandi?) is taking her cigarette break in the unkind dawn. She knows things. There's a Hallmark Christmas story behind every faded tattoo. Acting on a tip I scribbled punk rock lyrics in a foreign language I cannot recall. It definitely wasn't French. Not that classy not that tragic not that too cool for clown school. Gracias, Google Translate. I think it might have been Croatian.

spustila je to sranje bebe

i umrla sa mnom

jer je smrt jedina iskrena stvar

u ovom svijetu laznih noktiju laznih krizeva

ljudi vise nisu ljudi

zato je sve u pakao

umrijet cemo zajedno veceras

tvoj jezik u magarcu

Roscoe moze povuci okidac

probudit cemo se mrtvom dusom
u nekom raju maslaca od kikirikija
jeduci jedni druge za vjecnost

All the statues need to come down. Alice in Wonderland. Truman Capote. Jimmy Carter. Betty White. Gary Coleman. Betty Crocker. Whoopi Goldberg. Richard Burton. Strawberry Shortcake. Fuck them all. Who pays my light bill? Who wipes the shit from my ass? Who microwaves the water that becomes my instant coffee? Who fucks me gently with a chainsaw? Who buys my Slurpees? Who croons me to sleep? Who spoons the chicken broth into my delirious mouth and tells me I'm Snow White? I never was Snow White. Nor was I Rose Red. I was Ubiquitous Beige. It isn't hard to find a foundation to match my soul in the discount bin at Sephora.

When she heard the looking glass giggle she quivered with rage. She was a hundred times hotter than Angelina Jolie in "Gia"! The apple was ready so she painted her face and dressed up like a $20 whore and caught BART to the Tenderloin. The smug little bitch answered her door because she was idiotic and expecting Ken Doll. He was taking her to some hot shit sushi restaurant in North Beach because she sucked a mean dick. SURPRISE, MOTHERFUCKER! Instant muerte. But oh she died so goddamn pretty. Sadly, she was pregnant with Ken Doll's baby. All the little people grieved and remembered her over craft beer in her favorite Polk Street bar. Which songs did they play on the jukebox in the sad dead bitch's honor? Oh the usual. Anything by Sonic Youth. Anything by

The Mekons. Anything by The Smiths. Anything by Leonard Cohen. Anything by The Velvet Underground.

Troubling gender relations and meth induced rumors resulted in the bulldozing of Paisley Kindergarten, the hippest historical bar in downtown San Antonio. The martinis flamed. The fountains burbled ancient Aztec incantations. The hookers worked the back room like regular devotees of Isis. Pero. No mas. Now in its place another goddamn Gilded Monkey, like America needs another one of those. Gene Simmons is a financial backer. I mean of course he is. The smug son of a bitch. He's too prissy and vegan to come around. He's sober. He's clean. He stays home in his man cave in Malibu or wherever the fuck, counting stacks of crusty ass scented cash.

There's no subway in San Antonio so I ride VIA. That's the bus. The 100 Primo is my favorite. I get on that motherfucker and sit way in the back and close my eyes and enjoy the smooth ride, pretending like I'm Cher riding in her limo. Sometimes I sneak a drink from my Sunkist bottle. Of course it's never really Sunkist (what do I look like? A Beach Boy?) but Sunny D mixed with bottom shelf vodka. No one fucks with me. No one even tries. One glance at my tangled fucknest of long thick coarse bruja hair and motherfuckers know I'm not quite right. Do I have any regrets? I regret the discovery of my clitoris although if it weren't for sex with my purple elephant vibrator I'd have little reason to stay alive.

Bullshit. This has nada to do with me. I don't show up to throw away my little dutiful Texan American vote. I don't pay taxes. I don't buy lingerie. I don't buy yogurt and gluten free Cheetos at Whole Foods. I don't suck politician dick. I don't make babies. This isn't about me. This is a historical document informing future citizens about San Antonio, Texas, America. Shit got real.

Many motherfuckers, in short, were born. Many motherfuckers learned multiplication, division, English, Spanish, the Disney version of El Alamo, The Spurs, fat grams, carbohydrates, the politics of being sexually invisible, the politics of being broke, the politics of being brown, the politics of being white, the politics of being black, the politics of being stupid, Adam Sandler films, Wicca, poker, tarot, slot machines, the commerce of cunt, the fuck you all of dick, date rape drugs and self-care. Epsom salt baths. Soy candles. BREATHE in and out, baby, and let that shit go. Start your day with avocado toast and yoga. Room temperature lemon water. The water better not come from a faucet! Recycle, goddamn you! Collect cats. Donate to homeless shelters. FLOSS. Tip motel maids. They work harder than your mama. So. Yeah. Fuck yeah, as a matter of fuck ass fact. A lifetime of that bullshit a lifetime of that noise and then some kind of death and a casket and flowers and horrible organ music and half-assed eulogies. It's a movie starring Winona Ryder. It's a Billy Collins poem. Good luck finding a book of poetry that wasn't written by Charles Bukowski.

Mary decided to earn an honest living. She washed and cut and curled and dyed hair. We need more salons in our lives. Holly never did name her cat. She asks for opinions on her handwriting. Is she doing it right? Are her loops loopy enough? Gretel had to walk Adam's dog but wasn't counting on the crazy circus outside the tire shop. The silent man smoking the menthol cigarettes never gives anything away. He doesn't even own any books or dildos. Why is he even alive? He contributes nothing but derision and second-hand smoke. Jackson Pollock knew the shit ass score but was forced to scatter Cliff Notes around to gawking ass sniffers and mon-eyed morons. Yes YES That One Should Hang Over The Sofa And That One Of Course Over The Antique French Bed Oh Darling We can FUCK So GOOD To Those Wild Rainbowed Scribbles!

Tell them that the big outside world ain't so bueno, nothing to bleed for. Don't shame them for staying in their closets with their scented markers and Big Chief tablets. If you bully them into playing baseball and engaging in all those idiotic reindeer games you are nothing but a crab and by that I mean pubic lice. Plural. You are so goddamned plural, all of you. Don't mind me. This isn't about me at all. I'm the crazy eHarmony reject smelly on the futon cutting up magazines and Christmas cards and calling it art. I'm the flower, walled. I'm the handi-cap, stalled. I've got gall and guts and not much else. This is not a complaint. This is a history of San Antonio, Texas.

BUCK

Buck felt his balls drip sweat as he stood in the nauseating sunlight with all the other miserable and luckless citizens of Blue 548. The line was two or three miles long. Once they finally reached the food dome there would be more waiting but at least they would be out of the brutal heat. Guards stood at intervals with their assault rifles handing out plastic bottles filled with warm water. People swigged, puked. Some fainted. The sick were transported away in shiny blue vans. Blue flags emblazoned with 548 in matter of fact white font reminded the forgetful where they were. A lifetime ago Buck stood in a classroom each morning pledging allegiance to two other flags, both featuring the colors red, white and blue. One of the flags had fifty stars, the other only one.

"They love their flags on this planet," Truman said.

Truman was a voice Buck had been hearing in his head since he was a baby. At some point Buck named the voice Truman because he wrote a book report on the 33rd President of the United States when he was in the third grade. Like Buck, Harry S. Truman had been a Taurus. Unlike Buck, Harry S. Truman died long before the shit hit the proverbial fan.

The guard leered at Buck in his black sunglasses black t-shirt black jeans black boots. Oh he was "Top Gun" cool. He thrust a water bottle at Buck. Buck shook his head. He had taken his salt tablets before he left the trailer house at dawn.

"You got a death wish?" the guard drawled.

"Doesn't matter if I do or don't. Death will come for me when it's goddamn good and ready."

"Oh you're tough. John Wayne. Cowboy."

"Do you see a horse?"

"I see an asshole with crazy hair."

Buck decided the best policy was to ignore the guard. He was just another bully with a loaded gun. It wouldn't take much provocation for the guard to aim and fire. Slow day. Might as well kill a random citizen with a salty mouth and crazy hair.

The only law regarding hair was that it couldn't be dyed "unnatural colors." No bright reds, yellows, greens, purples, pinks, blues. A million years ago Buck had lost his virginity to a girl with bright pink hair in his dorm at Texas State University. She was dead now, according to social media. Jumped off a bridge into the Brazos on her fifty-third birthday.

Buck's hair was coarse and bushy and salt and pepper grey. He was glad he still had hair at fifty-nine. Few men kept their hair at any age in Blue 548. A lot of baldies running around, including the swaggering guard.

"All of this for a bag of groceries," Truman said.

The world had gone to shit and there was no one left for Buck to love. His wife and three daughters had been gunned down by a guard five years ago. His parents and siblings died of the virus several years before that. Buck was alone and didn't have much reason to stay alive but he stayed alive, anyway. And he still liked food, even the bland government issued food. Tabasco made it tolerable.

"Are we just here to stay alive as long as possible?" Truman asked.

Rhetorical question. The year was 2067 and the average life span in Blue 548 was 61. Suicide was the leading cause of death. Buck refused to kill himself because Truman had informed him and reminded him numerous times that his death would be more meaningless than his life.

"Stick around just to piss people off," Truman told Buck when he was staring down a bottle of pink allergy pills after the funeral of his wife and daughters.

But it was hotter than usual today and shit felt especially bleak so Truman wasn't up to the task of giving Buck another pep talk. Live. Die. Sweat. Be done with the sweat. Does any of this matter? Probably not. Maybe a group of angels or aliens or what the hell ever are watching it all play out, laughing, crying, applauding, yawning, scratching their celestial asses, munching buttered and salted popcorn, washing down the buttered and salted popcorn with cold Mexican beer. Ridiculous. Change the channel, already.

When Buck finally entered the heavily guarded and minimally air-conditioned food dome he fought the urge to remove all his clothing and roll around on the immaculate white and blue tile. A Richard Marx song from the good old days when

Patrick Swayze reigned supreme in the Hello Kitty hearts of prepubescent American girls blared from the speakers. "Hold Onto The Nights." Buck grimaced, remembering rolling a cart around Walmart in what was once San Antonio, Texas as that song played. Great Value mustard. Great Value ketchup. Great Value white bread. Great Value life.

"This song hasn't aged well," Truman said.

The sexually appealing apple scented synthetic service worker in the white and blue smock instructed Buck to place his left wrist under the scanner. Beep. Beep. Beep. Acceptable human. Acceptable citizen. Proceed.

"Congratulations. You get to stay alive. Please take your bag and exit," she said to Buck with an obscene neon red smile. She handed Buck a blue plastic bag bulging with groceries. Buck imagined grabbing the synthetic service worker's long fake platinum hair and biting her cool pale neck as he rammed his average but real penis inside her tight but fake vagina. The guards probably fucked the service workers on their lunch breaks. The idea of the fuckbots malfunctioning and pulverizing the meaty penises with garbage disposal vaginas made Buck smile deep on the inside.

So much for progress. We're still using plastic bags on this planet and the beauty standards remain idiotic. Oh. And we still don't have the whole sex thing figured out. Things are more fucked up than ever. Drugs and alcohol are illegal but television is free and as should be expected it's so much candy colored propaganda.

Buck dumped the contents of the plastic bag onto his candle wax puddled coffee table in the slutty glow of the setting sun. One jar of cockroach peanut butter. The cockroach fragments made the peanut butter especially salty and crunchy. The label made Buck smile. Black fuck you font on white paper. GOOD FOR YOU.

"I believe you, baby. I believe every word you say," Buck said.

A box of salty white crackers. Two green bananas. Six cans of SPAM. Three bottles of water. A bottle of Tabasco.

"We got a party up in this bitch," Truman said.
"You know it, amigo," Buck said.

Buck drank an imaginary icy beer. He toasted the setting sun and spoke a spontaneous poem.

"It always hurts to see you go. But you'll be back again, I know. How much night can one soul stand? Don't ask me. I ain't a boy band. I've never had anal but opinions vary. If I was a cow I'd own the dairy."

All this talent and I live alone in a rusting box. This is what Buck told himself as he lathered up with basic bitch white soap in the timed shower. Ten precious minutes of lukewarm water.

After the shower a banana and a bottle of water while watching the ancient boxy television set manufactured in Taiwan in 1977. Buck's favorite show. "Philosopher's Hour."

It was always the same set and the same two characters. An abandoned bar in the desert. A skinny Japanese man in a Free Food For Life t-shirt sat at a bar with a synthetic whore. The synthetic whore was always naked. She had long black hair, enormous black eyes and blatant red lips. She was pale with globular breasts and long slender arms and legs. Big ass. Flat stomach. Made to serve.

"Thank God and all his angels for Elvis," Lamar said. The man's name was Lamar Lincoln White. "Blue Moon" played on the jukebox. The synthetic whore's name was Sugar. Sugar smiled at Lamar and said, "Let's toast to Elvis, baby."

Sugar was sipping a glass of white wine. She seemed to be enjoying it. Lamar was guzzling Scotch on the rocks. He looked moody as hell.

"I shouldn't be drinking. When I drink I think. Thinking never did anybody any favors. Thinking is useless. Thinking doesn't solve a goddamn thing," Lamar said.

"I know, baby. I know."

"Let's fuck."

"Yes. Let's fuck."

Lamar fucked Sugar on the bar. Sounds were made. And that was it. An extreme close-up of Sugar's abnormally con-genial face. Elvis continued to croon. And that was a wrap. Perfection in ten minutes. Buck scratched his balls and turned off the television. He climbed into bed and fell asleep. He dreamed he was walking through the French Quarter with his wife on their honeymoon. They had spent their actual honeymoon in Dallas but Stella had always wanted to visit New Orleans. In the dream there was a fat orange moon in the sky and purple stars. Billie Holiday's voice was singing a Hank Williams song in some bar. *"The silence of a falling star lights up a purple sky. And as I wonder where you are I'm so lonesome I could cry."*

"Baby, where's the best gumbo in New Orleans? If you don't know I sure as shit don't know," Stella said.

"Let's ask that guy playing the saxophone. The way he plays that saxophone you know he knows where to find the best goddamn gumbo," Buck said.

They were holding hands, Buck and Stella, and they were young in the dream and better looking than Brad Pitt and Angelina Jolie. Buck kept telling himself, "Stay right here. Don't ever leave this dream world. This is the place to be. Stella. Stella. Stella. My Stella."

But then there was a siren. A raid. The humorless voice boomed through the bullhorn.

"All citizens come out of your residences. Come out immediately. Failure to comply will result in execution."

Buck opened his eyes. He could see the red lights through the filthy fly splattered blinds. Another goddamn raid. Buck gritted his teeth and wiped the tears from his eyes with his hands.

"What if I don't comply? What if I die right now? If I die can I go back to the dream?"

Truman was silent. Shots rang out. So many citizens were tired of complying. So many people were tired of being numbers. A man cannot live on cockroach peanut butter alone.

Buck started laughing and could not stop.

"This is your last warning. Lot twenty-seven. Come out now or face your death."

Die laughing. Die ebullient. Die victorious.

Buck did.

ELUCUBRATION

Two long glittering days later Sloth is alone in bed. The treasure map is stashed under a package of hashish. No job is too tough. To witness the certainty in a hurried fingers letter. Happy syntax. We belong to a fear-charged invisible America. The illusion of a one-tribe nation. Government officials strip the power from memory. Statues topple in conspiring swamps bloated with diarrhea diapers. The treasure map is stained and stashed two long glittering days later. Sloth is alone under a package of ramen. In bed alone no job is too tough. The happy syntax of a hurried fingers letter to the Fantastic Sam's manager. Witness the certainty of diarrhea diapers. The invisible low vibe tribe. The illusion of nation. The delusion of unity. Fear-charged wasp memory strips power from government officials. Statues topple because one straight week of triple digit temperatures and nothin' goin' on but the rent. Sloth, often thirsty, drinks alone. High up in an old-fashioned book with ivory pages the future shakes childhood's prayers from a miserable Virgo bride.

Hurts like a motherfucking bitch. Goddamn goddamn Sam's Choice I am. An electric blam inside Sloth's cellar head. Bruised on the piss soaked floorboards. "Find someone you can eat bacon and eggs with. Find someone you don't want to kill. Then you got somethin'." Uncle Buzz's Budweiser words. Got some cocaine but it ain't a Tarantino flick. Not quite that cool. A handful of subpar lovers and society's scorn. Scorched. Cannibalized mythologies. Adapting to a lifetime of rage. The electricity of ecstasy. Sordid centuries of fistfights and butt humidity with tender strangers across the toxic treasure map of the United States. Real is false and surreal is circus cereal. Define murder. The difference between murder in Texas suburbia and murder in the streets of Detroit. Define murder. Murder in a video game and murder in a Beverly Hills bedroom. Define American murder. Crystal meth fueled murder in El Paso. Purple lean fueled murder in Brooklyn. Prozac fueled murder in Alamo Heights. Dr. Pepper and allergy medication fueled murder in Atlanta. Slaughtered bank presidents and cops on bikes and Christian cheerleaders and animal activists. Furries convention. Oh no. Blood matted pink and yellow fur. Define murder in the American cinema. Define murder in the American shopping mall. Define murder in the bowling alleys of Wyoming. Define murder define homicide define suicide define Jack Daniels washing down Lithium to troubled bowels glutinous with Kraft macaroni and cheese. Ropes swinging from trees carved with the initials of cholas and their cholos.

Sloth wonders how his lips will weigh with quivering prayer. Forgiven. Delirious. Sloth's corazon is a con. Sloth's heart is an icon. Sloth's heart is a busted tape recorder. Chewed up greatest hits of Conway Twitty. Mangled greatest hits of Air Supply. Sloth seeks royal feet. Sloth implores a larger thing. Stripping in front of police officers Sloth resembled a Chicano that might be a real estate agent or owner of a furniture warehouse. Sloth looked like San Antonio. Sloth looked like hell yeah. Sloth the king of well-received and amplified blow jobs. Sloth the emperor of coffee ice cream and Cuban cigars. Exploited by white racist America Sloth is in dubious shape. The snake is red bellied the snake is white bellied the snake is blue bellied but at the end of the long glittering bloated ass shaking day the snake remains a snake that swallows us all.

Under a metallic sky Sloth turns down a muddy path. Needs a shave. Needs pleasing. Needs a woman well-versed in the vanilla arts. There is coffee to the right and whiskey to the left. Sloth keeps walking like the zombie actor in the $30 haunted house across from Tito's Taco Tuesday told him to eleven or fifteen years ago. "Keep walking forward, mijo! DO NOT STOP WALKING!" Sloth has lived his life by that clock that metric that rubric and now he is walking down a muddy path bloody and bruised and swollen and discombobulated yet resolute. Stoic, if you will. Anyone in America who isn't suffering from post traumatic stress disorder clearly isn't paying attention.

The girl's face was a slashed canvas brighter and more deeply saturated than any poppy. Obsequious democracy. Hail. Hail. More pop culture references than "Pulp Fiction." More issues than HUSTLER. Otherwise sensible citizens become the braying asses from Pinocchio as the Facebook Twitter Instagram machinery starts up its dull no sleep till Kansas City roar. All-around assholery. America's fatal flaw.

The undeniable power of the well-armed East Texas redneck. The power of the Apostle Paul quoting home owner. "Retain normal marital relations for that is what GOD tells us to do, damn it!" The power of the sex traffic pussy. OnlyFans or McDonald's? No brainer. For real, though. The power of the forty-seven year old woman and her twenty-seven year old cabana boy. The power of the purchase. The power of the quick trip to Juarez for cheap cigarettes and tequila and velvet Elvis portraits and silver snake rings.

Once on the Golden Gate Bridge Sloth looked down in his Faded Glory blue jeans a Marlboro dangling from his lips and said, "There are secrets deep and wide in the waiting room." But no one heard him unless they were psychic. All those cars and all those clouds and all those trees and all that water and Charles Manson still rambling and bad assing in prison dampening panties from Calabasas to Orlando. Elton John's sunglasses still defying dust and Velvet Jane's pussy pulsating with the Cherokee syllabary and vanilla frosted rainbow sprinkled donuts and blue xmas tree lights. Kiedis takes charge takes the wheel next stop Santa Cruz and Sloth gets kicked off the vampire karaoke stage for singing "Amarillo By Morning" ten times in a row.

"Sloth, baby, I'm gonna buy you a Mexican beer," the whore said. She reeked of blue cotton candy body spray and looked like Kevin Cronin on an especially harrowing day.

"Since when do whores buy beer?" Sloth asked, squeezing the whore's plump left tit.

"Since now, baby. I'm in love for the first time in my god-damn shit ass life, motherfucker!"

In the motel room they played SCRABBLE and the whore won. Her name was Kentucky. Sloth asked her if her great-grandfather fought in the Civil War.

"Bitch, please. I was born in 1984. My great-grandfather fought in the Jim Beam war. He lost."

"Look, baby. I don't want anything weird, dig? I'm a straight vanilla son of a bitch."

"So you want a half and half?"

"I like my coffee black."

"So I'll suck and ride your dick. That'll be $500."

"Who blew up my Twitter feed with that noise? Do I look like Bob Dylan?"

"You look better than that asshole. That's why I'm giving you a deep discount."

"Sweetheart. I've been around the paddy wagon block more times than you can count. Don't be fooled by my sexy Texas accent. I'll give you a Ben Franklin and buy your breakfast at the Cosmic Cat Café. Bueno?"

"If you want me to spend the night it'll be a lot more than that. I don't eat breakfast. I sleep in."

"Two hundred and my phone number. I'll be a repeat customer. I might even fly your butt to San Antonio for Thanksgiving. Love me some white meat."

"You got yourself a sugar baby, papi. Love me some brown meat."

Back in San Antonio Sloth dreamed of Kentucky. She was dressed as a genie. She told him she was there to obey all his wishes. She handed him snowballs of cocaine and sucked his dick until he melted. Then she ate the red licorice ropes she had tied him up with and they were together in the Pacific Ocean. Seals. Conspiring to stay alive despite sharks and tourists and plastic water bottles filled with cigarette butts and wads of sour apple bubble gum.

Six kilos. Pure. Top-grade. Johnny Depp never had it so good. Dreams up the Great Serpent the Mayan snake god. Kukulcan. Black pony voiced Johnny and his sweaty guns. Viewing room of one-tribe nation. The luxury of therapy. Let's discuss how you feel about Daddy leaving Mommy for a Cajun belly dancer. Switch. Flip. Static. Jupiter and Buddy Holly and Saturn and Patsy Cline again. The blonde in filmy pink. The brunette in 1975 orange. The soft glow of motel room rain lamp and the buzz of fried chicken porno television. Come back, Mister Information. Two more quarters. Lester Bangs slurping cough syrup spinning Question Mark and the Mysterians records. Bridget Fonda writhing to Marilyn Manson. Katie Couric bumping to Kanye West. Cameron Diaz grinding to Weezer. The blues translated by pay per view fuckbot. Choose Venus. Peanut butter extra crunchy on $20 trick cock. The tired and generic fascism of the Southern Baptist church. The glittering and vocal fried fascism of the U CAN'T TOUCH THIS one-percent. The wild chuckle freedom of poverty. Fuck me harder, fascist pigs. Spank that disenfranchised ramen ass. The giddy and godless freedom of the outlaw. Nothing to lose. Sweaty guns and sweatier cock. Black pony voiced motherfucker reading montage lines into open mic. Cannibal television. Cock blocked by CNN. Clit blocked by Fox News. Choose orange. Choose pink. Choose cock. Choose cunt. The luxury of choice. The power of I'll Tell You Later.

The sky was clear, hot, dull. There was no noise until there was and goddamn it was so motherfucking shit ass obvious. The lurking devil in the cerulean paint whispered, "Sloth you will defeat the desert, man." So Sloth painted and beaded sweat, blood, tears, cum until the rain came down like a bomb and washed away his motorcycle and he was busted flat with his brushes and a can of Ranch Style Beans. He knew how to construct a shelter from a Fisher Price box but he hadn't yet figured out how to pull a woman from his dreams and keep her, quite, in his arms. Plastic patterns. Legitimized oppression. Organic patterns. Reinforced oppression. The psychic terrorism of reindeer games. Denial of oppression. Ain't nobody here but us chickens. Sloth's brand of magick is rainbow kaoS. Fuck Wicca. Forget hoodoo. The rules are there ain't no rules. Create. Survive. Rinse. Repeat. Sleeping and slinging and singing and fucking and mucking and lucking and bucking the trends that would trap us all. Colored increaSe. Hued accordance. Abundance in cinnamon and anis estrellado. Dance with los diablos. Entranced but not enslaved by Santa Muerte.

"What are you offering?" La Flaquita inquired.

"Mi sangre," Sloth replied.

"Bueno. Quiero."

Banging fists in the ojo of rage. Glass splintering psalms. The Other World (El Otro Mundo) pouring from Sloth's head. Tumbling down centuries of controlled invisibility. Slashed wrists. Cliched agony. Soundless click. Furtive scratch. Floating across velvet abstractions. Elvis on Jupiter. Dan Zero on the moon. Andres Navajas on Mars. Stars bulging with escaped convicts and mass paperback antagonists and less thans.

Less than Kevin Costner. Less than Dana Plato. Less than Bill Maher. Less than Shannon Tweed. Less than Martha Stewart. Less than Eminem. Less than Hormel Foods. Less than Nabisco. Less than Nestle. Less than Ernie and the Keebler elves.

"I'm a less than," Kentucky told Sloth in the vanilla afterglow.

"You're a greater than," Sloth said, licking her raspberry nipples.

Cloudless energy of the forefinger and manic buzz of the clitoris and horses racing across Louisiana and Oklahoma and C.S. Lewis on Uranus and Lewis Carroll on Neptune and Alice in a John Lennon song and the walrus in a saturated slasher movie from 1981 and the brain on Paxil and the brain on Koyaanisqatsi and roast beef and ORGANIC TOMATOES and multiple orgasms and Barbie stealing pink high heels from Skipper and Ken on the boat which is Papaw's cowboy boot and once in Vegas Sloth saw The Most Beautiful Woman Ever Sponsored by Binion's and Mary Kay and he proposed marriage and she walked away like a peacock.

Dreams in Cantonese. Sweet apricot soap. What was done to you? What have you survived? Crying liquid eyeliner into cheap champagne. Knots in her strawberry blonde hair. Bruised breasts and puckered nipples and razor nicks on her legs and Sloth massaged her back and put his energy on her and in her and in the morning no breakfast just an hour in the boardwalk arcade and enough Skee-Ball tickets for a mermaid keychain.

The dunes dubbed algodones by the Mexicans. Lizard on a rock and voices in Sloth's ears. "There is no sleep in the canyon." Now the sun is singing. "Holy holy holy. Merciful and mighty. God in three persons. Blessed trinity." But the snakes in the sand know better as they hiss, "No tiene dominio aqui."

Dungeon's luxury of doubt. Surplus of lassitude. Dragon's share of ennui. Sloth drips sweat into the crimson paint in the desert sun, says, "Never met an Aztec I didn't like."

Bizarre sideshows inflamed with menopausal lust. Sloth pays $55 for the green tent. Burlesque grotesque with warrior paint. Too many feathers too many sequins too much gleaming beige flesh but Sloth chooses Chupacabra Disco Rainbow Queen and over Coca-Cola and corn dogs and Frito Pie she sho nuff shares her story.

"They named me Anna Lisa but I'm Gretel now. It's an

ironic name. I was born a Hansel. I've heard all the cheap jokes but I am every inch the Chupacabra Disco Rainbow Queen. Believe. Trust. Are you an Aries?"

"Nah. Capricorn."

"You must have Aries rising."

"I have dick rising."

"Oh, honey. Tell me more tell me MORE."

"Mucho mas, mamacita?"

"Si. Mucho mas, papi. Por favor."

"Well. Since you asked so nicely."

The water was running and the candles and incense were lit. Miles Davis. Soapy and languid in the honeymoon suite jacuzzi Gretel sucked Sloth's cock until vanilla rainbowed into caramel with boysenberry with dark chocolate swirls. Blabbering blurbing nation of zombies. Tribe of zero. Social media saturation and filtered selfies and Sloth is coming home inside an hour that is a melted and congealed century. All the paintings have paid off. At last. At last. Sweet Jesus at last. Fruitful tuition. Frenzied tablature. Eargasms.

"It's more a spiritual practice than anything else. When I'm painting I'm praying but I'm not asking for any favors and if I have an audience it isn't participating."

"You don't paint for money?"

"You got jokes. I paint for gold but it's no kind of currency in this climate. You can't steal it."

"I want it! I want GOLD!"

"Get to minin', mija."

Paid in fractured syntax. Paid in ecstatic snippets from recalled and rejuvenated 1971. Paid in telenovela. Paid in mangonada. Paid in piano. Paid in surreptitious toke. Paid in papaya. Paid in sun and moon and asteroids and constellations and the Rio Grande and the Wichita Mountains and bus ride from Tucson to Fort Worth. Paid off in Capricorn midheaven. Paid in one night at La Quinta Inn. Paid in one night in Eagle Pass. Paid in casino coffee. Paid in circus orgy.

Animated glamour attached to TikTok cuties. Power dolls. A white girl appropriates picadillo con papas. A brown girl appropriates white cream gravy.

"The oppressed cannot appropriate. Everything within reach belongs to the oppressed. If you're disenfranchised you're disenfranchised. Ancestry.com ain't got shit to do with it."

"No comprende."

"I'd like to appropriate those $500 Fluevog shoes but that shit ain't happenin'."

"There's always Payless."

"Fuck you."

Hypersensitive microphone at the top of the blue cowboy mountain. Grillos en el monitor de video frio. Sonidos de voces lejanas. Throbbing unwanted gift. Cobbled together with gristle. Ah man. You're my babe and don't you dare forget it. It's Monday all the time and recess never comes. The less than minions croak, "Reprieve!"

The cunning killing of an unarmed man. It's all Barry Ma-
nilow's fault. Blame Bruce Springsteen. Blame Ronald Reagan.
Blame baby powder. Blame Mommy. Blame Daddy. Blame
Wolverine. Blame last year's plumber. Blame tomorrow's aes-
thetician. The mortician won't know the difference.

Riding Greyhound drunk with a sullen stagnant feeling
Sloth made up a song that summed up the loneliness that was
a canyon that was a planet that was a Color Me Badd song
that was a galaxy yawning between himself and all of yesterday's women.

chemistry sorting demon
critical switch
instant pussy
dripping bliss
sipping seas of tequila
still can't forget
last wishes
all those salty kisses
down on me
shadowed symphony
and now I'm dead and now I'm free
and none of this matters
goddamn The Platters
just one more corazon
throbbing raw
nah dawg I'm good
I'm good
in the Dollar General hood

The mermaids sing oh so obscene and peachy keen beyond the bony reach of the poetry spouting pirates. Sloth's eyes are glazed donuts. If he can conjure up Candy he can have her all the time. But what is time but a thimble and what is love but a cactus. Desire is the ax that fells us all. No one hears anything but their own spastic heartbeat in this forest of the damned. Oh but Candy was sixteen and Sloth was twenty. Libra girl. Capricorn boy. Serenades on a duck park bench. Sex in the San Antonio tangential lollipop noche. All grass and moan and quiero quiero quiero. Mucho.

Fucking madness, vanilla or no. The celebrity elite. Reality televised. Sociopathic billboards. Obscene poetry. Obscene because it grinds us all to almond meal. Nothing feels louder than a text message at two a.m. "U up???" No. I am down. Down down in pinot noir town where a fuck possesses much more gravitas than a paper plate heaped with Velveeta nachos. Suck a fuck. Deeply fucked and deeply unknown. Candy shone surplus cinema and every woman since has been a glorified hand job.

Sloth sits like a statue that hasn't been toppled yet on his stool at the Texas T.

"You look just like that cop," horny white woman slurred.

"Que? You got me all wrong, baby doll," Sloth said. He banged on the bar for another Tecate. Dolores was slow.

"You know. From that tv show."

"Oh. Yeah. You're right. That's who I am. That's where I'm from."

The horny white woman's name was Leslie Dawn Whittaker. Sloth reminded her of Erik Estrada from "CHIPs." She wanted very badly to suck Sloth's dick but he was thinking about Nadia from two or three years ago and Leslie wasn't his type, anyway, because she had a trendy Karen haircut and no discernible tits. Also. No discernible ass.

The questions are bologna sandwiches and the answers are buffalo. The chicken shit killing of an unarmed man. It's all Robert Plant's fault. Blame Geraldo Rivera. Blame George Bush. Both of 'em. Blame Tylenol. Blame gingerbread. Blame gumdrops. Blame Rudolph the Red-Nosed Reindeer. Blame Frosty the Snowman. Blame Bugs Bunny. Blame last year's orthodontist. Blame tomorrow's birthday clown. The mortician won't know the difference.

WE'RE ALL MACHINES

"Graham, I got a story."

"Good morning, Jimmy. I don't have any time for nonsense. We go to press this afternoon."

"You can run this in next week's issue. You don't want to miss this."

"Come to my office."

A map of Texas hung on the wall behind Graham's desk. Graham was proud of his roots. Seventh generation Texan. His great-grandfather created The Wise County Chronicle in 1919 on his ranch in between Bridgeport and Decatur. Now it was 2019 and Jimmy Ingalls, the town crazy (the town is Bridgeport, one-hundred miles southeast of Seymour), has a story. Graham humors Jimmy because Graham is crazy in his own way, with Mars conjunct his sun in the eleventh house and Mercury in the late degrees of Aquarius. He doesn't want to miss any goddamn thing. Hebrews 13:2 has always been Graham's favorite verse in the King James ("if it ain't King James it ain't right," Graham's daddy always said). Be not forgetful to entertain strangers, for thereby some have entertained angels unawares. Word. Jimmy could very well be an angel.

"Bobby Bailey is working for the Illuminati. I seen him burning evidence in his front yard, talking about spider blood. You know they require blood sacrifice. Well, Graham, I am worried about the children. It starts with insects and animals and then it progresses to humans. Usually children because they are easy targets. You know his girlfriend Angie works at Pizza Island. I believe the puppets are spies for the Illuminati. It's all connected, see?"

"Bobby Bailey is a retired rodeo clown living on disability. I think the Illuminati could find better representatives. The puppets are animatronics that sing Buddy Holly songs. If you take the animatronics apart you will find wires. They're machines, Jimmy. Now I've got to get back to work. I've got a paper to run."

"You're better than that, Graham. You ain't a sheep. You got a good mind. You know the truth. The truth is…we are all machines. We are all being programmed. Haven't you noticed the water tastes different lately? Haven't you noticed the sun and moon don't look the same? Haven't you noticed the planes sound eerier than usual? My only hope is that we can find a way to debug ourselves before it's too late."

"What happens when it's too late, Jimmy? Armageddon? The Tribulation?"

"Oh, worse than that. Come on now. This ain't Vacation Bible School. It's gonna go down like this, more or less. The Illuminati will take over. We will have to have a chip implanted in our left palm in order to survive. You wanna go to Walmart's and get groceries? Without the chip you will be shit outta luck, excuse the vulgarity. We will all be slaves programmed to eat our own pets and children. Eventually we will be sent to Mars as guinea pigs. God help us if we wake up inside that day."

"Okay, Jimmy. I'll keep an eye and ear out."

"Man, you are patronizing me but that's cool. I know what I know and I will continue to know it. You got my number. Give me a holler when the shit hits the fan."

"Will do."

Jimmy walked across the street to Dodi's Donuts. The gal behind the counter didn't speak the best English but she was a great listener. Kim Wu. Her name was Kim Wu.

"Same donut as every time?" Kim Wu asked Jimmy.

"Yeah, honey. Three chocolate and two glazed. And a large cup of black coffee, please ma'am."

Jimmy sat down at his usual table near the counter. He blew on his coffee and looked around. No one else in the shop.

"Kim Wu, I gotta tell ya. These are dark times," Jimmy said.

"Dark times? This is day. Sun shining," Kim Wu said. She was sweeping the floor in front of the counter. She wore her long black hair in a ponytail. Her t-shirt was bright red. Jimmy wondered if Kim was a Buddhist or a Muslim. Maybe she was a Communist. Atheist.

"Let me ask you somethin'…just curious. You ever go to church, Kim Wu?"

"I go to Church of Christ with husband, yes."

"So you're a Christian? Good. Well, when the bad stuff, the really bad stuff, starts to happen you'll be okay. I mean we will inherit paradise, after all. Us Christians. Jesus promises us that much. Sure, there will be some unpleasant things to go through but if we can just hang tough we will make it to Glory."

"Bad stuff? I don't know. Everything pretty okay."

"Sure, things seem pretty okay right now. We got the sun, although that's a topic for another day, and donuts and coffee. We can still go to church and worship as we please. We can go to Walmart's and Family Dollar and buy all that we require to survive and even enjoy life to a certain degree. You ever heard of the Illuminati?"

"Um, no. Never heard."

"Don't worry about it, hon. Just don't ever go to Pizza Island. The puppets are spies working for the Illuminati, a group of really evil people. People. I say people. They aren't people. They're monsters. I hate it for the kids because kids love pizza and singing puppets. I tell the parents to boycott the place but they don't listen. Everyone loves the pizza. Best sauce ever, they say. Make your own pizza at home! Great Value frozen pizza ain't that bad! No sir. Too lazy. And I guess even the parents enjoy the entertainment, if you can call demonic singing puppets entertainment. Me personally I'd rather stay home and listen to some George Jones or Merle Haggard on the radio or watch 'Hee Haw' reruns or play with my dogs. But what do I know? I'm old school. Could I get a refill on the coffee, please ma'am?"

"Sure, Jimmy. Singing puppets not a nice idea, I don't think. No need to go to Pizza Island. We stay home or go out for fried chicken only sometime."

"Kim Wu, you are one smart cookie."

"Cookie? Cookie can be smart? You say things, seem weird. Weird things. Evil puppets and cookies that think."

"Fair enough. The English language is weird, I guess. We make up these weird little sayings to pass the time, make life more interesting. But the puppets really are evil. That ain't wordplay. All I mean is, you are smarter than most people in this town. Doesn't matter if you can't speak English very well. You are definitely intelligent and perceptive. And I am very glad to know you are going to Heaven when you die."

"Not dying for a long time, Jimmy. Alive. Happy. Feeling good."

"Amen to that, sister. Amen to that."

Dodi appeared from the kitchen. Jimmy raised his cup of coffee in greeting. Dodi glowered.

"Jimmy, stop pesterin' Kim. She's tryin' to work. Don't you have some rows to hoe?"

"I hoe my rows at the crack of dawn, Dodi. I ain't pesterin' my good friend Kim Wu. We're havin' an important conversation."

"I bet you are. I don't wanna hear no more crap about Pizza Island or the Illuminati. Those fear tactics ain't welcome here. If you keep it up you can shuffle your butt on down the road to Yum Yum Donuts. I'll ban your butt quicker than a rooster on a rat."

"Ban me? From this place? Dodi, I would be ashamed. You've known me and my family for years. My nephew played flag football with your son. How dare you speak to me that way? After all the donuts and coffee I've bought over the years."

"I don't care about none of that. I'm old and I'm worn out. I've lost my tolerance for crazy talk. You can run your big mouth somewheres else. I've had my bellyful."

"Jesus, please forgive Dodi. She don't fully realize what she's sayin'."

"If I need forgiveness I'll be the one to ask for it. Take that talk to Reddit or Discord or the YouTube, damn it."

"Jesus loves you, Dodi."

"Oh hell. Who doesn't he love? He loves us all. Hallelujah."

"Yes he does love us all. You're right about that. And I guarantee ya you will be praying extra hard when the Illuminati sets the hounds of hell loose on this town. I'm prepared for that day. You obviously are not. My apologies, Kim Wu. I'm terribly sorry you had to hear this ruckus. I'll be on my way now. I hope you have an excellent day."

"Thanks, Jimmy. Please be okay. The sun is shining."

"Seems to be shining, true. Bye, Dodi."

"Scram."

"I would be ashamed."

"I wouldn't."

"Queen of the last word. You just really take the cake. More fun with the English language. Wheeee. Okay, Dodi. You win. I lose."

When Jimmy was gone Dodi shook her head and took a swig from her bottle of water. It was hotter than hell in the sugar dusted kitchen. Kim Wu put away the broom and washed her hands.

"I know you are polite and kind-hearted, Kim, but you don't have to listen to Jimmy's nonsense."

"Nonsense, yes, but Jimmy needs to say a few things. No harm, really. We can smile, pretend to understand."

"You're a much better woman than I'll ever be."

"No. Not better. But Jimmy is a sad man. Things not so clear in his mind."

"You're right. I don't know why I snapped. I'm just tired of hearing about Jesus from people who never knew the guy. Bottom line, Kim, I'm tired of all the crazy talk."

"Crazy talk. Yes. So crazy, all the talking."

HELL IS HOBBY LOBBY ON BLACK FRIDAY

The blood rushed from Everest's pussy, hot and thick. The clots of menstrual blood on the maxi pads looked like jelly. Started when she was twelve. She knew she was expected to be excited, like Judy Blume's Margaret. Everest was not excited, enthusiastic, ebullient, overjoyed, triumphant. She didn't feel like celebrating and singing to the world HEY BITCHES!!! I'M A WOMAN NOW!!! She didn't feel like thanking God. She felt like crawling into a hole and dying.

"You're on your way now," her mom said with a wry smile.

"What the hell is that supposed to mean?"

"I was so happy when I got my first period. It means you can have babies now."

"Yeah, I saw the film two months ago. I guess I should blow up pink and blue balloons, maybe make a batch of Betty Crocker cupcakes."

"You know to wait until you get married. When you start dating you can kiss and hold hands but that's as far as it goes."

"I'll never go that far. No one will ever want to kiss me. Just look at me."

"You're beautiful now and you'll get even more beautiful."

"Bullshit."

"Why can't you be sweet like your sister?"

"She's too stupid to know how fucked up things are."

"Go to your room. I will not tolerate that kind of language."

"Don't expect me to start speaking Chinese."

Everest was standing in line in the cafeteria. She was wearing her new Guess? jeans and pink and yellow ESPRIT shirt. The white chicks sitting at the cool table (they all played tennis and wore Swatches on both wrists) started giggling and pointing. Yes, Everest was white, too, but these girls were really fucking WHITE. Tennis. Multiple Swatches. James Avery jewelry. They had names like Brooke and Meagan and Heather and Allison. Whenever their parents were in Europe or The Virgin Islands or wherever the fuck they had parties in their sweet little two-story cul-de-sac McMansions, drinking wine coolers and getting felt up to Bon Jovi and Def Leppard ballads by white boys with names like Bryce and Jason and Liam and Chad. Someday these special little bitches would own the free fucking world. The cool table. Everest would never be allowed to sit there.

She sat alone at the end of the table taken up by the brown kids. Latinos. Latinas. Chicanos. Chicanas. One of the brown girls looked at Everest and said, "Hey! Sierra or Emerald or whatever the hell your name is. You know why everyone is laughing and pointing at you? You got blood on the back of your shirt. You need to clean that up. That's disgusting. We're trying to eat here, pendeja."

Everest stood. Walked up the brown girl and grabbed her hair. Yanked hard.

"The name is Everest but you can call me Reyna, bitch."

When Everest was thirty-seven she celebrated her life as a white woman by getting a hysterectomy.

"Are you sure about this?" Dr. Green asked.

"I'm sure."

Dr. Green was a Christian, mother of six. Framed pictures of her children and grandchildren filled her office. She could not conceive of a woman choosing not to have children and choosing to have a hysterectomy when she still had the chance to meet the right man and make at least one baby. She knew Everest's medical history (hospitalized twice with menorrhagia, lost more than half the blood in her body both times) but she didn't know Everest's mind. Few did. In Everest's mind only idiots chose to bring babies into an increasingly more cacophonous fuckscape. And she was damn tired of bleeding. Goddamn. All the stains. All the humiliation. The cramps.

"I know. I know. I am such a pussy. This world ain't my playground," Everest told nobody.

"Girl, you is a rock star," nobody said with a high five.

Seneca Diane Finley Robertson, Everest's only sister, sits across the table from Everest at Thanksgiving and says, "You aren't depressed about it?"

"Depressed about not having a uterus? Can't say that I am."

"Well, I cannot even begin to imagine. I cannot imagine not being a mom."

"You don't have to imagine. You are a mom. And when exactly did you think I'd decide to start having kids? When have

I ever given the impression that I wanted to get married and pop out babies?"

"It's just so extreme and so final. I just…I can't imagine."

"Don't try."

Seneca and her husband Kevin were the proud parents of four healthy, noisy children. Max. Mickey. Maci. Mindi. Max and Maci were Aries. Mickey and Mindi were Gemini. Seneca didn't believe in astrology but Everest had found it to be valid. Everest could imagine and it hurt. All that noise all the time. Seneca often reminded Everest that Jesus wasn't cool with astrology, tarot, witchcraft and women who choose vibrators and books over husbands and babies. Gay people? No bueno. All on the highway to hell.

"Hell is Hobby Lobby on Black Friday," Everest told Seneca.

"Whatever. I love Hobby Lobby," Seneca said.

Everest was thankful for cheap chardonnay. She drank six glasses then passed out on the denim sofa in Seneca and Kevin's media room. Great color scheme. The walls were painted a faint suggestion of sky blue. This color calms crazy people, according to legend. And the pillows on the sofa were indigo and the carpet on the floor was grey and the abstract paintings that hung on the wall were cerulean and white because minimalism was trending.

"The less we say the better," Connie liked to say. Mercury was in Aries when Connie was born but it was conjunct Saturn in Connie's second house. Everest liked to call her mother Connie most of the time. It just felt more honest. Daddy was Gary, a man Everest hadn't spoken to since 1991.

"Gary, I'm flat ass broke," Everest said during the phone call.

"Uh, I'm Dad. And I'm sorry about that, kiddo. I can't help you out. I'm going through a helluva divorce right now. Krissy is really taking me to the cleaners. I don't have two nickels to rub together."

Everest…kiddo…earned her wings on the streets of San Francisco. Having an older boyfriend didn't help. Lynx wasn't exactly a sugar daddy. When he wasn't rocking the stage with his band Holly Valens (influences included the Red Hot Chili Peppers but only circa "Freaky Styley" and the Butthole Surfers) he was schlepping around the offices of Purple Mountain Majesty Press, a small publishing house. Lynx tried to help Everest get a job there but she flunked the interview. No one seemed to appreciate Everest's low energy deadpan personality. Most people weren't sure she even had one.

No uterus. No personality. A bitch cannot win.

"It's your super brain, baby. You intimidate people. You're a seventeenth century German philosopher trapped in the body of a twentieth century native Texan," Lynx said.

"I appreciate your faith in me but that doesn't help. I guess I'll do sex work."

"You're in the right city for it."

The peepshow in North Beach was called Bestial Baby. Everest showed up to the audition wearing a pink lace slip and fuzzy pink slippers. All the other hopeful whores were gothed out in black leather and fishnets and bondage collars.

"It's all nude," one of the girls told Everest in the dressing room when she was wondering if she'd worn the right thing.

"All nude?"

"Well, you can wear your fuzzy slippers. Those are cute, by the way. So retro. You didn't know this was an all nude joint?"

"No. I'm from Texas."

"Ah. I'm sorry."

Everest said that a lot ("I'm from Texas.") by way of apology and explanation. I'm sorry I'm such a dipshit. I'm sorry I don't know the lay of the land. I'm sorry I said the wrong thing. I'm from Texas, y'all. Oh. We get it. We get it. No worries. You are forgiven.

As Everest danced on the narrow enclosed stage with the goth chicks to the throbbing techno music she hoped her pubes and nipples and face and hair and fingernails and slippers would be deemed acceptable. The men sat at the peepshow windows staring with no expressions on their faces. Were their dicks hard? It was hard to tell. There was no heat to their eyes. It was brutal but Everest survived and to her disbelief she passed the audition.

She made most of her money in the private rooms. Her most faithful customer was an old man who went by Horse.

Apt. He had a huge cock. Everest's stage name was Silk. She wanted to make it as easy as possible for the johns. Silk. Slides right off the tongue. One easy syllable. So easily moaned.

"That's so good, sweet baby. Silk. Oh Silk," Horse moaned as Everest sucked his cock. He caressed her scalp with his gnarled fingers and Everest made appreciative slurping sounds.

"It must get confusing for you, baby, keeping up with all those names," Lynx said with a laugh. They were in bed wallowing in the afterglow, drinking wine and listening to Lynx's favorite Coltrane record. "A Love Supreme."

"Just keep callin' me Baby, baby. I like that name best."

"Does it weird you out that I'm not jealous?"

"Jealousy is retarded. You can do sex work, too. San Francisco is the most democratic city on the planet. Anyone can be a whore."

"Las Vegas may argue that but I'm talking about jealousy, not envy."

"I know. Jealous of what? An old man and various sad weirdo freaks paying me to suck their dicks and piss on them? There's no heat. No fire. Well, that's not true. Sometimes I get turned on. Okay, I get turned on a lot. I'm a depraved slut with sun and Venus in Aquarius. But groove is in the heart and my heart is mired in your mud."

"God, I love how you word things."

"We're so compatible. It's sickening."

They kissed like they meant it and fucked again as the hot wax spun and the moon waxed oh so bodacious in Sagittarius.

ARACHNID BLOOD

Angie woke up and stumbled into the kitchen, rubbed her eyes. Bobby was frying bacon and scrambling eggs, singing "Family Tradition." He raised his can of Budweiser at Angie and grinned. Angie poured herself a cup of coffee and sat down at the table.

"You're happy," Angie said.

"Yes ma'am I am," Bobby said, placing a plate in front of her.

"This must be Christmas. Or Easter. Or the Fourth of July. Some damn thing. Wait. Did you finish writing your book? Is that what this is about?"

"I finished writing my book. Yes. It is finished. Let's eat and then I'll read it to you. It's so damn good I could just shit myself."

"Don't do that. But this is the best news I've heard in forever. Baby, I'm so proud of you. Do you think you'll be able to sell it?"

"I doubt it. Maybe I'll publish it myself. I don't know any fuckers in New York or L.A."

"You should at least try to sell it. You should talk to the guy who runs the newspaper. Graham what's his butt. He probably knows a publisher."

"Hell, I don't need his damn help. I can get on the internet and find someone if I want to sell it. But right now I feel too damn good to set myself up for rejection. I just want to bask in this glory. Mama would be so happy for me."

"Yes she would. So would your daddy."

"Maybe. Daddy never really cared too much about books. Or about me, for that matter. Daddy just lived for the rodeo. He's the reason I was a rodeo clown. I wanted to impress him. Didn't work. I hope you like it."

"I'll love it because it came from you. I love your brain, baby."

"Thanks, baby. I love your brain, too."

"I think you love my tits."

"Of course I love your tits. I love all of you."

Angie washed the dishes then washed and dried her hands and sat down on the laundry strewn sofa in the den and picked up the manuscript. Bobby sat down beside her and cracked his knuckles.

Arachnid Blood
by Bobby Bailey

Zed knew there was something that set him apart from the other kids his age. He was thirteen. He didn't care about video games or action figures or comic books. But there was something more than that. His dreams were so vivid each night it was almost as if he was living a separate reality. In his dreams his name was Jasper Johnson and he had superhuman strength. He could pick up cars and trucks and throw them over a bridge. He could crush skulls with his bare hands. He could also teleport, read minds, see perfectly in the dark, and climb walls.

In one of his dreams a skeleton approached him and told him to sit down. Jasper Johnson sat down on a rock. The skeleton paced around. He had something important to say.

"Jasper Johnson, you have been chosen," the skeleton said.

"Chosen for what?" Jasper Johnson asked.

"You are going to be a hero to many. You may not know this but you have heroic DNA. You have what is called arachnid blood. Your ancestors came to Earth from another planet from another star system thousands of years ago. All aliens are different. These particular aliens, your ancestors, are similar to arachnids. You will have to poison people in order to survive. But be careful who you poison. Only poison those who are useless. Do not poison those who can actually help you. You want to spin metaphorical webs."

"Metaphorical webs? What are the webs metaphors for?"

"Connection. You will poison those who are useless, those who would destroy you if they could, and create connections with allies. The connections are about love and power. You can have both. It is a common misconception on Earth that you cannot have both. You can. You can have powerful love. You can be empowered by love. It will be the work of a lifetime, figuring out how to be selective with who you poison and who you love. It will be the work of a lifetime to figure out how to love yourself enough to empower yourself. When you wake up you will need to remember this dream. I will show you numerous signs to help you remember. Wake up now, Zed. Remember. You are Zed but you are also Jasper Johnson and you are special because you have inherited arachnid blood."

When Zed woke up he looked in the mirror. Everything seemed the same. He had brown hair and blue eyes. He had a decent nose and an acceptable mouth and a regular chin. He was tall for his age. He had a strong body because his father owned a boxing gym. He knew how to throw punches. As Zed stared at his reflection a tiny black spider crawled up the mirror. Zed had always been afraid of spiders so he grabbed a paperback book and slapped the spider dead.

As Zed walked to school Spider-Man zoomed by on a motorcycle. Zed told himself it was some weirdo in a costume. He laughed. Then in first period the teacher, Mrs. Parker, introduced a new girl to the class.

"Class, this is Mary Jane Watson. She just moved here from New York City," Mrs. Parker said.

Mary Jane Watson sat down at the desk in front of Zed's. She turned around and asked Zed if she could borrow a red pen.

"Why red? I only have blue and black pens," Zed said.
"Oh. Too bad. I'm drawing hearts with drops of blood."

After lunch Principal Ditko made an announcement on the

intercom. There would be an emergency assembly in the auditorium immediately. Zed found his friends Tony and Norm. They sat in the back row so they could play games on their phones in peace. Zed wasn't really interested in video games but he pretended like he was so that he would have something to discuss with his friends. He wanted to fit in. He didn't want to stand out like a freak. What was Zed actually interested in? He didn't know yet.

"It has come to our attention," Principal Ditko said from the podium, "that spies have infiltrated the student population. These spies are leaving cryptic notes. They do not speak our language. I do not wish to alarm you but these spies are aliens from a star system too far away to be detected by NASA. These spies look like ordinary American teenagers but they are far from ordinary. Why are they here? Simple. They are gathering evidence. The evidence they gather and take back to their home planet will be used by their leaders to determine whether or not Earth is worth saving. If they determine that Earth is not worth saving they will destroy us within the next decade. For some of you that is fine. You don't want to continue living, anyway. Many of you are in counseling for assorted problems. C-PTSD. Depression. Anxiety. Many of you are struggling with suicidal ideations. Good news. You won't have to go to the trouble of finding a gun and ammo, figuring out how to make a noose and hang yourselves or hoping that you have enough Benadryl and Jack Daniels to get the job done. If the aliens determine that Earth is worthless you won't be around much longer, anyway. You might be around long enough to be able to get your driver's license , vote, obtain cigarettes and alcohol, maybe have sex for the first time, maybe get a job at Taco Cabana or Kohl's or T-Mobile or Verizon or Foot Locker or Hot Topic. But for those of you who want to live for at least a few decades on this planet, you are going to have to get to work. Give the aliens every reason to believe that there is hope here, that there are signs of intelligent life, that this planet is indeed worth saving. Show up. Be exactly who you are. If you're gay, be gay. If you're straight, stay straight and don't be ashamed because you prefer the opposite sex and are okay with the pronouns that were assigned to you at birth. If you don't like video games, don't play video games. If you don't enjoy porn, don't look at porn. If you masturbate, don't feel guilty about it. The aliens can pick up on guilt and shame. They abhor those vibrations. Guilt and shame are in fact strikes against the continuation of this planet. The aliens are disgusted by guilt and shame. Guilt and shame do not exist on their planet. They want to see excitement, exuberance, ebullience. They want to see your eyes shining with life. Some of you seem like zombies to these advanced beings. They look at you and wonder…why do these beings even stay alive? What are they doing down here? They are dead inside but think they are alive simply because they are breathing. These advanced beings are not being cruel or judgmental. They are sincerely confused. They see you walking around with your faces buried in your phones. They are not seeing webs of connection. They wonder if some of you are machines. And if you are in fact machines, what are you being programmed to do? They fail to see the point of your programming. Students, I implore you. Get excited about something. Anything. Walk into class and tell your teacher you just saw the most amazing sunrise. Tell your best friend about a painting you saw in a museum or better yet, tell your best friend about a painting you created your goddamn self. I apologize for the language but I'm getting emotional here. I know there are many things to hate about this planet but there are more things to love. We had the Vietnam War. That was terrible. We had the Holocaust. More horrible than any horror movie. Mass shootings. Serial killers. 9/11. My wife works for CPS. I know the evil that is done to innocent children by their own parents. Spiders. Someone is dying right now because of a damn spider bite. Again. Excuse my language. I am tearing up. Snakes. Same thing. There are many snakes that are so venomous they will kill you. Not because they hate you. That's not how snakes operate. They are just created that way. They contain venom and if they feel threatened they will bite you and you could die in agony. Tornados. Hurricanes. Wildfires. Earthquakes. Tsunamis. Drunk drivers. I get it. Life on this planet often sucks so hard you don't even want to get out of bed and try. But I am telling you to try. Try because Wrigley Field. Try because Spider-Man. Try because Green Goblin. Try because New York City. Try because San Francisco. Try because Tokyo. Try because Basquiat. Try because Jackson Pollock. Try because Janis Joplin. Try because Jimi Hendrix. Try because Otis Redding. Try because Billie Holiday. Try because one day or night your parents decided to have sex and you are here and you are proof that love and lust exist. You are proof that at some point a couple of people got excited about something. If you were conceived via IVF, same thing. Your parents spent a lot of money on getting you here. In short, students, each of us are the result of two people trying so we should honor that effort and show some effort of our own. Show up. Try. Get knocked down in the mud. Get up. Try again. Love. Love. Love. Love like your life depends on it. It does. Love so hard that it hurts, students. That is the only way this species can survive. Be sure to drink your Ovaltine."

Zed jumped to his feet and clapped his hands with tears in his eyes. Soon every student in the auditorium was standing and clapping. Earth would be saved.

In the hallway Zed yanked on Mary Jane Watson's long red hair. She spun around with fire in her eyes.

"Are you trying to piss me off?" she asked.

"Yes. Well, no. Not exactly. I was just trying to get your attention. I'm Zed Zenner and I find you obscenely attractive. Would you like to join me for dinner on Friday night?"

"You were inspired by Principal Ditko's speech. I was, too. Yes. I love hamburgers."

"Me, too."

That night the skeleton came to Zed again in his dream. The skeleton transformed into Andrew Garfield. He was wearing an Oakland Raiders jersey and gold chains.

"You done good, dawg. Yo. Know what I'm sayin'?" Andrew

said, bumping fists with Zed.

"I guess you're complimenting me. You're proud of me. But why?" Zed asked.

"You showed up. You were yourself. For real, though. Just sayin'. You like literally saved the motherfucking planet. I told you…you're a hero. You got that arachnid blood, playa."

"I thought Principal Ditko was the hero. I just asked out the new girl."

"Nah, man. You don't get it, bro. You are the principal. It's that metaphorical web I was talkin' about. Connection. You are Principal Ditko and you are Mary Jane Watson and you are me and I am you. Comprende?"

"No."

"You'll get it eventually. You are well on your way. Peace out."

For the rest of Zed Zenner's life he used his great power with great responsibility. He didn't feel the need to climb walls or throw vehicles off bridges or crush skulls but he love love loved like his life depended on it. He loved himself. He loved his blood. He loved his ancestors. He loved his parents. He loved his cousins. He loved his aunts. He loved his uncles. He loved his grandparents. He loved his friends. He loved his teachers. He loved his girlfriends. Mary Jane Watson was Zed's first girlfriend. Not his last. Zed moved to Tokyo after he graduated from high school and worked with a team of similar geniuses. The general idea was to promote fierce and fearless love on a global scale. Soon all organized religions and weird new age cults were obsolete. Money was no longer a thing. There were no countries no flags no military. No submarines. No tanks. No guns. There were still knives but they weren't used to kill people. They were used for practical purposes, such as cutting up a steak. People used their phones to call people. That was it. No more Google. No more Facebook. No more YouTube. No more Twitter. No more Instagram. Families hung out together on porches singing and playing instruments. People got together and built bonfires and sang and danced and roasted marshmallows. There was no casual sex. There was only intense sex. If you liked someone well enough to get naked with them you had intense conversations and the intense conversations led to intense sex. People only married people they had excellent synastry with. Someone with a first house Scorpio moon would not dream of marrying someone who had a twelfth house Libra moon. If you could not communicate telepathically with a lover there was no reason to continue the relationship. People read books, discussed books and wrote books. There was nothing sexier. People looked at art, discussed art and created art. Nothing sexier. People listened to music, discussed music, danced to music and created music. Nothing sexier. There was no suicide. People caught onto the fact that they were spirits having a human experience. No reason to abort the mission. They would all return home soon enough. Abortion was legal all over the planet but people rarely had abortions because people were more conscious of their choices. Few people committed rape. Few people had random mindless sex. Most people who did not want to procreate used some form of birth control.

Some people abstained from sex altogether. They didn't desire it. Serial killers were no longer glamorized. There were fewer serial killers and fewer killers in general. Fewer psychopaths. People were just better all the way around. They thought better and felt better and loved better and looked better and smelled better. No one was interested in Keeping Up With The Kardashians. Who were these mythic Kardashians? Some forgotten clan from a lesser time.

When Zed Zenner was on his deathbed at the age of one-hundred and fifteen his great-great grandson, ZuZu Zenner, sat down beside him and asked him to sum up his life in two or three sentences.

"Oh, I'll need more sentences than that, ZuZu. You could sum up my life in one sentence, actually. I loved the whole goddamn ride. Yes. Make sure they carve that on my headstone, please. I loved the whole goddamn ride. Were there some bumps on the road? You bet. Did I get scratched up and beat up and bruised up and bloodied up? Yes. Yes. Yes. Yes. But I said yes to all of it. I showed up. I didn't hide. I ran out to greet the day like it was made just for me, like I was five years old and just seeing the sunrise for the first time. I offered up my heart to the gods of surprise. That's all any of us can do, finally. We are here to offer up our hearts to the gods of surprise. Goodbye, my boy. Remember. You have arachnid blood. With great power comes great responsibility."

As Zed Zenner breathed his last breath his face lit up and he smiled. He saw something no one else could see and he was glad to see it.

Angie looked at Bobby with tears in her eyes. Bobby's lips quivered.

"Oh Bobby. That's the greatest story I've ever read."

"You really think so?"

"Oh yes. I want to take this to the newspaper right now. This should be published immediately. Everyone in the world needs to read this."

"Well, everyone in the world won't read it if it's published in our little rinky dink newspaper. Maybe I should put it up on Facebook or maybe I could create a YouTube channel and read it in a Spider-Man costume."

"No, read it like yourself. People should see your eyes. People should see your tears. But right now I want to celebrate. I want to buy a bunch of balloons and set them free."

"Mama would be so proud."

"Let's go to the cemetery and read the story to your mama."

"Nah, she ain't there. I'll light some candles tonight and read to Mama from right here. I know she'll hear me."

"I just can't get over how good this is. I want to share this with the world. This could help so many people."

"I'd like to think so. Well, it helped me just writing it down. I feel like a weight has been lifted off my shoulders. I said what I needed to say. I expressed what I needed to express."

"This could be a Marvel movie."

"It ain't formulaic enough, sweetheart. Not enough action. But I'm glad you like it. I guess I was worried you wouldn't get it."

"Oh I get it. Our planet is in peril. We need more love, less technology. We need to destroy the matrix. Get back to the basics. Like your parents. When they met and fell in love they didn't have any of this noise. I wish we could have lived back then when everything was so beautiful and basic."

"Let's don't glamorize the past, baby. They had their problems. I wouldn't want to live through the Great Depression. Let's get excited about the future."

"You've got a point. Come on, let's drive to Scotty's Liquor Barn and load up on party supplies then go to Dollar Tree and get some balloons."

"That's a plan."

The first song on the radio when Bobby started up the truck was "Kawliga." The original version. Bobby laughed and shook his head.

"Thanks, Daddy. Gotta love synchronicity," he said.

"Your daddy's favorite song?" Angie asked.

"One of 'em. And I was singin' a song by Hank The Original's son earlier in the kitchen."

"Oh yeah. I remember. Synchronicity is the damnedest thing."

CLOWN GRAVY

Vanilla Cupcake was talking shit again, talking about how she would give anything to get in my bed for one hour. One hour is all it would take. It ain't nothin' nice bein' the only African-American in a circus full of wack ass crackers. Sometimes I drop my g's. Nothin'. Bein'. I'm from Killeen, Texas. Fuck y'all. But I'm educated. I know how to talk like the white man. I only drawl when I have to. The thing is, I'm not some ignorant asshole selling balloons and cotton candy. What I do takes talent and balls. I'm a circus clown. The circus is in my blood. My parents were trapeze artists. My mom ran off with a German tourist. She still sends me Christmas cards from Berlin. My dad drank himself to death. I tend to keep to my damn self. Only woman I ever gave a damn about was Sugar Delicious. Best trapeze artist since Lillian Leitzel. She wore the hell out of those sequins. But Hollywood snatched her up and now she's married to some hot shit producer and they have five perfect kids and two or three houses. She was up for an Oscar a couple of years ago.

But Vanilla Cupcake is lookin' better and better. Sleazy chick. Wears too much makeup even when the tents are down and we're all just chillin'. I guess she thinks she's got somethin' to prove since she ain't nothin' but a concession stand chick. She overcompensates with the dirty talk and the drinking and the drugs. Wants the world to know that she's as tough and sorry as any man.

"When you gonna let me have a taste of that lollipop?" Vanilla Cupcake slurred, leaning toward me at the card table and giving me an extra close view of her ample cleavage and a whiff of her cheap body spray.

"I ain't got no lollipop," I said, puffing on my Cohiba and studying my hand. I didn't have shit. A ten of clubs, a five of diamonds, a two of spades, an ace of hearts and a king of clubs.

"Oh, since when? Did Sugar bite it off?"

"Don't say shit about Sugar."

"I'll never be rich and famous. I'm so sorry. I'm just a circus peasant, same as you."

"You ain't nothin' like me."

"You think you're too good for me?"

"Nah. It's the other way around."

"Aw, that's the sweetest thing you've ever said to me, cookie wookie."

"It's too soon for terms of endearment. Look, go get me a Coca-Cola for my rum."

The stupid thing is, Vanilla Cupcake took off to fetch me a Coke. Buster laughed and shook his head, threw a handful of peanuts in the center of the table. He thinks he's the biggest bad ass of us all. Fifth generation circus clown. Has a scar on his left ankle he likes to show off. A poodle bit him once.

"Vanilla wants some of that clown gravy," Buster said, chomping on his ice.

"Oh is that what she wants? I thought she wanted a lollipop," I said.

"You do realize that 'lollipop' is a sexual euphemism, right? She doesn't want candy, Jammo. She wants dick. Specifically, she wants yours."

"Oh gosh. Oh gee. I can't believe that flew right over my head. Thank you for the education. Should I fuck her, man? Should I use a condom or just pull out? Or should I just let her suck the gravy from my lollipop? All these white people metaphors confuse a motherfucker."

"Shit, Jammo. Get your panties out of that wad."

"I ain't got no panties, sweetheart. Gave my last pair to your mama."

"Stop talking shit and show your cards."

Buster was real proud of himself like he had anything at all to do with the pair of eights, three of clubs, four of clubs and five of clubs he slapped down on the table. I slapped my cards down and said, "Fuck this bullshit. Drink that Coke for me." Buster laughed. He was pretty damn pleased with himself for a man who had just won fifteen peanuts. I headed for my trailer, looking forward to another Friday night of internet porn and bottom shelf rum.

Then a black cat crossed my path and by black cat I mean bad fuckin' news. Talk about bitin' a dick off. If anyone is capable of such barbarity it's Empress. She's the witch of the circus. Reads cards and palms in her spooky little tent. I've never been into astrology or the occult or any of that bullshit but I know a bad vibe when I feel one. I've never exchanged more than the basic courtesies with the lady. She looks at me with those green eyes like she wants to devour my soul.

"Jammo. I have something I need to discuss with you," Empress said. She was just wearing a Jimi Hendrix t-shirt and raggedy shorts but she spoke to me like she was true royalty and I was some random errand boy. I wasn't havin' it.

"I don't think so, Empress. I'm just makin' my little way to my humble little abode for the night. It's been a long day. I'm about ready for some shut eye."

"This won't take long. It's rather urgent."

"We're acquaintances, Empress. I don't invite acquaintances inside my home."

"I understand. But I really must insist. You'll understand why soon enough. This conversation requires privacy, I'm afraid."

Empress wasn't afraid of shit. I looked in her green soul devouring eyes and could discern that she was power tripping. But our world is small and I didn't want to piss her off. She meant serious fucking business. I acquiesced.

She sat down at the small table in my kitchen and I offered her a glass of water. She shook her head. I sat down across from her and hoped she would get right to the point. She didn't disappoint.

"I was reading my cards tonight. It was a private, personal reading. The full moon is in Scorpio, right on my sun and Mars. But a voice told me, 'This message is for Jammo.' I drew the nine of swords. Okay. Maybe it was a fluke. I shuffled the cards. I got the nine of swords again. I shuffled the cards again. I drew Death. I've never given you much thought, Jammo. I know you don't like me. I avoid people who don't like me. So, as you know, I spend a great deal of time alone. But we're in this shit show together and I do care about you in an abstract kind of way. And I received this message and could not in good conscience fail to deliver it to you. Do with it what you may."

"I don't believe in all that mumbo jumbo. Scorpio. Mars. Swords. Death? Yeah, we're all guaranteed one of those. Shit show? Yes ma'am. I was born into it. You know my history. I'm the only black man in a low-rent circus. Everyone makes it a point to know my business. I ain't known nothin' but shit my entire life, which is why I'm a clown. I hide my misery behind cheap paint and entertain kids and idiots for just enough money to stay alive on this miserable hunk of dirt. I see that you're sincere. I appreciate your concern. But I'm going to show you to the door now and ask you to relay this message to that mysterious voice: White ain't always right."

I loved the look on Empress's pale face at that moment so much that for a few crazy seconds I thought about apologizing to her and offering her a glass of rum. The mask dropped and I saw a lonely, vulnerable woman. She kind of reminded me of a less beautiful and much less assured Ava Gardner.

"I'm sorry for bothering you. You're correct. White ain't always right. Goodnight, Jammo."

I really felt sorry then. She was lonelier than I was. I knew she'd been married once before she joined the circus. I'd heard a vague rumor about a daughter she placed for adoption when she was a teenager.

"Empress, I'm sorry. It must have been difficult for you to approach me."

"Yes. It was. I knew you wouldn't believe me. But as I said, I had to relay the message."

"I was just about to put a pizza in the oven. It's just a frozen pizza. But would you join me for dinner? I've got some rum."

"No, thank you. I'm careful about what I eat. And I don't drink. But I appreciate the offer."

"I truly am sorry, Empress."

We stood at my door really looking at each other for the first time ever, I guess. Lonely white woman. Lonely black man. Two misfits and outcasts thrown together in the chaos of circumstances. There's music to the universe if we listen. Fuck. Now the bitch was in my head. What is the word "bitch"? It's a dirty old penny. It jangles in my mind with other dirty old coins. Cracker. Cunt. Whore. Skank. Slut. Trash. Nigger. Those words ain't no kinda currency but that is what we know and that is what we exchange even without speakin'. All of us. Human beings. Rats and cockroaches, all.

"So am I," she said.

"Can you read me? I mean…beyond the obvious?"

"Yes."

"You seem tentative. Be bold. I need you to be bold."

"It doesn't matter what you need me to be. I'll be exactly what I am. I see that you realize the truth, suddenly. The truth is, I am not superior to you. The truth is, Jammo, we all wear some kind of paint. You saw me without mine. You were afraid of me before. Now you know that I have my stories, just as you have yours. This is all basic. It isn't brain science or rocket surgery. But we forget. We walk around in survival mode. We say and think the bare minimum. You have a few people you banter with. I don't even have that. I don't think you pity me. You empathize with me."

"That's right. I do."

"Just be careful. I don't want to see you come to a bad end."

"Can you see my death? Do you know when and how I'll die?"

"I'm feeling shaky. I need to sit down."

"Here, sit down on the couch. I'm sorry I don't have anything to offer you."

"It's fine. I'm impossible. I'll tell you what I see. You can dismiss it if you want."

"Tell me. Please."

Sitting beside Empress on the couch I felt closer to her than I'd felt to any other human being in years. Her hands were shaking and there were tears in her eyes. I reached for her hand. She looked into my eyes as she squeezed my hand. I wasn't afraid of death, not really. I'd always kind of anticipated it. I just wanted to be close to her. I savored the intensity between us. I was so used to cardboard interactions with everybody else. Finally some blood, some real flow.

Then there was a banging on my door. Fuck. I jumped up and opened the door to find Vanilla Cupcake. She was furious with her red face. Her breasts were heaving. She had never looked more appealing. She held a cup of Coca-Cola in one hand and a bottle of rum in the other. She looked past me to Empress sitting on my couch.

"Oh so that's what you want? You want a fucking witch bitch?"

Vanilla threw the Coca-Cola in my face. I laughed and she hurled the bottle of rum at the wall behind me. It landed un-broken in Empress's lap.

"I seen y'all talkin' and knew the score. I could predict this soap opera from a mile away. You don't need no special powers to predict this shit," Vanilla seethed.

"Honey baby, you don't shit about shit," I said.

"What the hell is that supposed to mean? She's sittin' there half-dressed on your damn ratty ass couch. I'm bustin' some-thin' up. Fuck it. I'm done. I'm over it. Hope she don't put a voodoo curse on ya."

I closed the door and threw up my hands.

"Women. I can't please none of y'all," I told Empress.

"Jammo, I see you getting in a car with Vanilla. Don't," Empress said.

"Well, as you know I don't own a car and neither does Vanilla."

"I see you and Vanilla sharing an Uber to a bar. You don't make it to the bar."

"Why? Is the Uber driver drunk? Does he crash into a tele-phone pole? Do we all die on impact?"

"There's a head on collision with a drunk truck driver. You and the Uber driver die on impact. Vanilla survives but is in a wheelchair for the rest of her life."

I couldn't help it. I busted out laughing. Life doesn't make any damn sense. It's just so goddamn absurd, all of it. My name is Jammo and a woman named Vanilla Cupcake wants to seduce me. The only woman I ever loved is a rich and famous actress. And a lonely witch named Empress wants me to stay alive so I can entertain kids and idiots for just enough money to keep pizza in my freezer and bottom shelf rum on my table. Maybe she wants to seduce me, too. Hell. Why not? Everyone wants that clown gravy on their lollipop.

"Baby, we all gonna die," I said, sitting close to Empress and putting my arm around her. She recoiled from my touch and made a face. That was it. I was through. Maybe there was some magic between us and I fucked it up with a cheap move. She wasn't my kind. There was no reason for us to exchange anything deeper than a "take care."

"I said what I came to say. I'll go now."

"Wait. How much longer do I have?"

"It isn't a diagnosis, Jammo. You can avoid it."

"Maybe I want to get in an Uber with Vanilla. I'd like to

get laid before I die."

"So you plan to have sex in an Uber with Vanilla minutes before your death?"

"Sounds like a party. I'm game. Why the hell not?"

"You're just another garden variety moron. You'll get laid tomorrow night."

"I don't turn you on?"

"No. I have a strict no assholes policy."

"I don't like assholes either. I'm all about the pussy."

"Then you'll die reeking of Vanilla Cupcake's. Enjoy."

"Thanks, baby."

I fell asleep laughing that night. Uber, hell. The nearest bar is only two blocks away. Mickey's Club House, it's called. Best damn jukebox in town.

BACON

Love's function is a clown smirk. My mirror gives me decembriated statistics. In today's gelatinous meat market I'm not worth very much. I'm forty-six years old. I don't possess a uterus or a cottage or a BMW or a stellar pair of pillow tits. My legs could be longer. My hair is a fucknest. Jammo Pie Greasepaint, the man I loved most, has been dead for a week. Bunny called me yesterday to give me the news.

I only had sex with Jammo once and it didn't go very well. This was back in 1983. He was thirty. I was fourteen. He popped my cherry. Even though I was drunk on peach wine coolers it hurt like hell. We met at a carnival. He was actually a circus clown but he had friends who worked the carnival and he was helping out. I was there with my friends, slutty in my Vidal Sassoon jeans and ripped ESPRIT shirt. I thought I was hot shit in my blue eyeshadow and pink lipstick. Jammo thought so, too. We did it in Bunny's travel trailer while Bunny was working the Zipper. I remember "China Girl" was playing on the radio. We fucked through several songs but "China Girl" is the only one I can recall. Jammo kept calling me Baby, telling me how good I felt.

He seemed surprised by all the blood. He pretended like he thought I was eighteen and experienced. We shared a joint after and talked about religion and politics and cartoons. I fell in love immediately. He wasn't like the guys I knew from school and church camp. He was smart and had lived a hard life. And he was black. I was just a spoiled white chick from suburbia. My dad was an attorney and my mom was a chef. I didn't know shit about shit. I thought I wanted to be a choreographer when I grew up. Anyway. We kept in touch. Exchanged snail mail for a few years. Then I found him at MySpace and he was all about some chick he'd met in the circus. I thought they'd get married but she left him for some Hollywood asshole. She's a famous actress now. Hangs out with Nicole Kidman and all those other mannequins.

I've been married and divorced three times. I didn't love any of my husbands, not really, not for any length of time. I was always co-dependent until a couple of years ago when I finally got my ESL certification. Now I'm in San Antonio teaching high school kids how to speak English. I live in a shitty apartment across the street from Planet Fitness, Taco Bell, Popeye's, Whataburger and Fallas Paredes. I don't have any pets or kids, just a vibrator and a fuckton of books.

So Jammo died in Tahlequah, Oklahoma. Cherokee Nation. How appropriate. He told me his great-great grandfather was full-blooded Cherokee. He died in an Uber with this flaky Vanilla Cupcake chick. She worked the concession stand at the circus. Head-on collision with a drunk truck driver. Everyone died except for Vanilla. She's in bad shape, though. Bunny says she'll probably be in a wheelchair for the rest of her life.

"Did Jammo love this Vanilla Cupcake bimbo?" I asked Bunny.

"Nah. They were just friends. They were taking the Uber to some bar called The Lion's Roar."

"Bunny, I would have liked to attend the funeral."

"I'm sorry. It wasn't much. He was cremated. We scattered his ashes in Lake Tenkiller. But I'll send you all the stuff I found in his trailer that has to do with you. All the pictures and letters and books you sent him."

"I'm glad he still had all that stuff. God. I loved him."

"I know. He loved you, too."

"Bullshit. Oh I guess he was fond of me. But that Sugar Delicious bitch is the only woman he ever loved. I don't guess she was at his memorial service."

"Of course not. She's in Italy making a new movie with George Clooney."

"How fucking fabulous."

"You sound really bitter, Angie."

"I am. I move like a robot through dooms of love."

"What does that mean?"

"Nada. It's my self-pity mixed with e.e. cummings."

"What's that?"

"He was a poet."

"You and poetry. Jammo said you always talked over his head. But he said it with love in his voice."

"I'm sure he did. Thanks for calling, Bunny."

When I got off the phone with Bunny I lit some vetiver incense and my fat purple candle. Turned off all the lights and sat on my futon smoking a bowl, drinking a glass of prosecco. I couldn't see Jammo without seeing Sugar Delicious. Those pictures he posted at MySpace made me sick with envy. He looked so lovesick. I don't think I've ever made a man lovesick. I closed my eyes and thought of the phone call we'd had years ago when I was in rehab. I was nineteen and strung out on coke. Jammo told me, "One monkey don't stop the show." That never really sank in until my third marriage ended and then I lost my mom to breast cancer. Who the fuck was I if I wasn't Jim's wife and Laura's daughter? I was lost at sea trying to doggy paddle my way through a hurricane. I wanted to die. I've always wanted to die. But that was the closest I've ever come to death. I woke up in the middle of the night when I was forty-four years old covered in my own vomit, courtesy of Jack Daniels and Benadryl. I thought of Jammo telling me with a chuckle over the phone, "One monkey don't stop the show." Who was going to clean up my vomit? Not Jim. He was fucking Cheryl. Not my mom. She was under dirt. So I cleaned up my vomit and more or less got my shit together.

Sitting on my futon by the glow of the lone purple candle in my weed and wine haze I heard "Hey Joe" playing in the apartment downstairs. That was Jammo's favorite Jimi Hendrix song. The tears traveled all the way from my eyes to my breasts. Jammo sent me this beautiful letter once after I got out of rehab the second time. I read it so many times I committed it to memory.

Angie Sweetheart,

When are you gonna stop this bullshit? You're a goddess, baby, so stop pretending like you're a clown. I'm a clown. A black circus clown, no less. You think the world will ever bow down and kiss my toes? You're white. You're educated. People love you. Start acting like you've got some sense. You're the smartest woman I've ever met. You were a woman when I met you even though you didn't know it because you were distracted by all that MTV shopping mall teeny-bopper gossip bullshit. I'll never forget looking into your blue eyes and hearing you denounce Jesus in your sweet little Texas drawl after we had sex. I guess I should feel guilty about taking advantage of a virgin but I never have. You were beyond me and above me in so many ways. I could never love you the way you need me to love you because you elude my comprehension. You're as spacious as the sky, filled with stars that don't need names. The stars shine on all of us and I think that might be enough. That's what we got, darlin', so let's deal with it.

Love & Smooches,

Jammo

I told Jammo he could be a poet if he wanted to be one. He didn't want to be a poet. He wanted to be a clown. I went through a phase where I thought I was the next Sylvia Plath. I even self-published a book of poetry. *Gooey Chocolate Corazon.* I dedicated it to Jammo and sent him a copy. He called me up one night and asked me to read the entire book to him over the phone. I did, hoping he'd fall so deeply in love with me he'd propose marriage. That didn't happen. But he appreciated my effort.

"If a man tells you not to love him you should obey. That's just his way of telling you nicely that he will never love you," my mom told me once when I was confiding in her about Jammo. I guess Mom knew the score. She didn't know the details about Jammo, just knew he was a man I'd always pined for. But Mom collected men like they were dolls. Married and divorced six times. Before she got sick from all the chemo she was dating a plastic surgeon named Vince. He wasn't there when she was dying, didn't come to the funeral, didn't even send a goddamn bouquet of flowers. But they had only dated for a couple of months.

Cock. Cunt. Dick. Pussy. First kiss. Last kiss. Marriage. Divorce. Booty call. Hook-up. Casual sex. Fling. Unrequited love. Hickeys. STDs. Pillow talk. Phone sex. Instant message sex. Text sex. Fucking, Screwing. Roleplay. Eating ass. Anal sex. Sucking dick. Spanking. Fantasy. Prostitution. Porn. What the fuck does it all mean? It's all nada. It's all Motown.

God. The songs. My mom was always playing what I like to call wrist slashing records when I was a kid. "Three Times A Lady." "If You Leave Me Now." "Sad Eyes."

I grew up believing in the white American heterosexual mythology sponsored by Coca-Cola and Rolex. Luke & Laura. Bobby & Pam. Bo & Hope. Oh to be so lucky. To be so known to be so adored. Love that looks good on camera. Love with a soundtrack. Love that lasts.

I guess I'm bitter because I stopped believing in the lies

and believed in something else when I met Jammo. Who the fuck could write our story and call it true love? The American audience would not accept our story as the gold standard. And of course it wasn't because it didn't turn into a big church wedding and a two-story house on a cul-de-sac and two kids and a sailboat and happily ever after. People would dismiss what we had as shabby, common, vulgar. Black alcoholic circus clown devirginizes white spoiled teenager in a travel trailer during a carnival. It wouldn't even work as a porno.

Bunny sent six packages bulging with photographs, letters, birthday cards, books. I sat in my bed in my panties and a SPAM t-shirt Jammo sent me for my twenty-first birthday surrounded by the evidence of my ridiculous love. Pictures of me looking sultry. Pictures of me looking silly. Pictures of me looking wistful. Poems about our one night together. Poems about our telephone conversations. Poems about the two of us getting married and living in Fiji. I know I was projecting. Tripping, as Jammo would say. "Girl, I was only your first fuck. Ain't you had better dick than mine?" Jammo asked me once in a late night phone conversation when I was begging him to come see me. It wasn't about sex. He knew that. I just loved him. And he loved me but not enough to do anything about it.

He did plenty. There was mutual exchange. If we had gotten married maybe it would have fallen to shit. Of course it would have fallen to shit. Two addicts in love. Age gap. Cultural gap. Blah yada blah. We weren't no kind of Nora Ephron script.

Soursweet unknownness. Heaven duly notified. Daunting green mountain. Skull bashing sky.

"Baby, I'm sitting here eating bacon in the nude watching the towers come down. Damn it, Jammo. You should be here holding my hand. Your hand is the hand I want to hold when towers are falling down," I wrote in a card with Snoopy on the cover. Right after I put the card in an envelope and sealed it the phone rang. It was Jammo.

"Baby girl can you believe this bullshit? I was just fryin' up some bacon to go with my Bloody Mary when this mess blew up my damn television," Jammo said.

"I just ate some bacon and wrote you a letter tellin' you I was eatin' bacon in the nude."

"Bacon in the nude? Crazy woman. Now I'm scared and turned on at the same time. So I guess you think this means we're soulmates."

"Nah. I think it means we're a couple of bacon lovin' motherfuckers."

Jammo laughed then and that's the secret to everything and that's what I loved the hardest and will miss the most. That man's laugh. If that man's laughter wasn't music if that man's laughter wasn't pure joy then music and pure joy do not exist and everything in this motherfucking world is a motherfucking lie.

AMERICAN MEOW

My country tis of huh? I don't understand what the hell "tis of thee" means. I keep meaning to Google it but I get distracted by boobs, butts and Budweiser. I am an American. I identify as an American cat with a proclivity for anonymous sex and sour apple wine coolers. I didn't ask to be born in this country. I kind of just was. They say you're hanging out bored in the spirit realm and you look down and try to find the most appealing sexually busy couple. While this appealing couple is engaging in sexual intercourse you plan your existence. You wait for the appropriate moment and then will yourself into your mother's womb. She'll give birth to you if she doesn't miscarry or have an abortion or get killed while you're growing in there. I doubt the validity of this theory. If it's true a lot of spirits made some sorry decisions. I certainly did. But I don't think I had any say in the matter. Because as I stated previously, I identify as an American cat. And the truth is this: I was born an American human male. I don't mind being male. But I mind being American and human. Allow me to expound and hopefully elucidate.

Since I was a child the English language has confused and depressed me. My first word was MEOW because I found the family cat more fascinating than my parents and siblings. I spoke to Truman. He spoke back. I still speak to Truman and he still speaks back even though he has been dead since I was four years old. I am now thirty-three years old. Truman remains my best friend.

I was born in Tulsa, Oklahoma during an F5 tornado on April 17, 1999. Right after I was born the lights went out. I don't recall any of this. My mother has told me all this several times. My birth has been one of the most exciting moments of her life. My mom is quite ordinary and boring. Barely graduated from high school. Married my dad who received his GED. My dad made his living as a plumber and drank quite a bit. He's a vegetable rotting in a nursing home these days. My mom always just took care of me and my five siblings. Cooked. Cleaned. Worked in the garden. Made sure we went to church each Sunday. First Baptist Church. Now she lives in the house I grew up in. I live there, too. It's not an ideal situation. But we manage.

Human relations have always proven to be quite the challenge for me. I don't appreciate how most humans communicate, obviously. I prefer to speak cat. School was a struggle. I did manage to graduate from community college only because the instructors could tell that I am brilliant. They did not like me but they had to admit I was not an idiot. I am surrounded by idiots but I like to have sex so I pretend to enjoy the company of women.

I lost…well, lost is the wrong word…I gave my virginity to Samantha Bridwell when I was twenty and she was fifteen. We met at church. She sang in the choir and I watched her. I appreciated her boobs and butt. Her face was acceptable. I invited myself to her home after church one Sunday for supper. I told her father I was interested in helping out with the livestock in exchange for a pittance. He didn't have any sons so he accepted my offer. So yes, I was sneaky about it. We did it three or four different times in the barn. By "we" I mean Samantha and I. I enjoyed the sex but wasn't crazy about my partner. Samantha wasn't crazy about me, either, fortunately. No hearts had to be broken.

After Samantha I had a brief fling with a woman I met in the grocery store while shopping for food for Truman. Even though Truman, as I said, was no longer living, I still bought (and indeed, still buy) food for my friend and leave it in a dish behind the house so my mom doesn't know what I'm up to. She would not approve. "Um. Why don't you do the normal thing and just buy a new cat?" I know what you're thinking, see. Because you are normal. You might even be sane. Well, to be curt, fuck you. You've never loved anyone or anything like I love Truman. I'm sorry if such love and devotion eludes your severely limited understanding. If you do understand, I apologize for insulting you.

The woman I met in the grocery store is not important. Her name doesn't matter. She could have been anyone. She could have been your sister, daughter, mother, girlfriend, ex-wife, a prostitute with a personality disorder and a drug addiction. You get the gist. We only had mediocre sex on two different occasions. I don't exactly think of her whenever I hear "How Deep is Your Love?" or "Hard Habit To Break."

All the sex I've had since has been anonymous. You know what anonymous sex means. I go to this club. There's Marilyn Manson music. All kinds of beverages and drugs. I usually stick to beer and cocaine. I see a woman who appeals to me. I grab her by her hair and whisper, "Meow meow MEOW" in her ear. She isn't an idiot. She knows exactly what I mean. We go to what I like to call Fuck City. It's a little room with a battered purple loveseat. We fuck on the loveseat. After orgasm has been achieved we go our separate ways.

This is what I hate about being an American. I hate how we are media saturated and obese. You'll pry those Fox News babbling iPhones and Ding Dongs from our cold dead hands. We burn witches and other outcasts (I am speaking in metaphors, please forgive me) and crown the hollow heads of the facile and the socially adept. Kardashian Nation. We like our guns. We like our cops. We like our fast foreign cars. We like our cheaply made porn. We like our Disney Pixar movies. We like our unfunny sitcoms. We like our morally bankrupt soap operas. We like our idiot chatter talk shows. We like our airbrushed celebrities. We like our meaningless bar trivia. We like our war machine. We like our propaganda. We like our Home Depot. We like our Walmart. We like our coupons. We like our caffeinated beverages and donuts. We like our cracker box houses. We like our brand of religion. God The Father. Jesus The Son. Holy The Spirit. Casper The Friendly Ghost. No American ghosts are friendly. I hate to be the one to break the news to you, amigo. American ghosts speak in blood and smoke signals and guttural cries. American ghosts MEOW.

Yes. MEOW is usually friendly. But not always. I'll tell you what Truman conveys to me. Each MEOW is different. Here is a recent exchange:

I say to Truman…I say…Truman, I'm so tired of living down here. People are deplorable. And Truman says meow… meow…MEOW…meow? Meow. Meow meow meow meow MEOW!!!

Translation? If you insist. By that Truman simply means, "Yes. I know. But you think stuff is bad now? Wait. Wait until you die and all is revealed. When you enter the spirit realm you fully realize how completely depraved, idiotic, horrible and pointless life in America truly is."

So. Something to look forward to. At least when I'm dead I'll be with Truman and other sensible ghosts. I'm struggling lately. I'm struggling to hold onto some decent shred of sanity. How do I cope? Other than visiting with Truman and indulging in anonymous sex with appealing women in Fuck City? I read books I don't comprehend, such as anything by Gertrude Stein, Kathy Acker and William T. Vollmann. I read Mexican comic books. I don't know Spanish. I fantasize about being an actual cat, the kind that prowls around and eats mice and garbage and has cat sex on hot summer nights beneath a fat leering pervert moon. I create cat collages all over my room and bathroom. My mother has Jesus art hanging in the kitchen and den.

What do I eat? Tilapia and tuna, mostly. I don't eat sugar.

My mother tries to tempt me continuously with her peach cobbler and vanilla ice cream and biscuits with grape jelly and sugary iced tea and pecan pie and tunnel of fudge cake and powdered sugar donuts. She finally stopped making birthday cakes for me because I always refuse to eat them. My mother is a typical American. Yes. She has diabetes. She still has all her limbs, though. Her teeth? She lost those decades ago. She has dentures, of course.

It's safe to say I'll never procure employment, get married, make human babies, buy a house and a truck and a tractor and a bunch of animals and stick an American flag in my piece of dirt. The American government does in fact send me a check on the third of each month. I make $790 a month for being depressed and anxious. I'm not on any meds. I tried Paxil once. It rendered me impotent and constipated so I quit cold turkey after one month of misery.

The psych ward. Yes. I've been there on three different occasions. I've tried to kill myself three times. American suicide attempts are so banal. They are mostly cries for help. I wasn't crying for help. I was trying to get to Truman. The first suicide attempt occurred when I was thirteen. I was tired of being lonely and bullied at school. I washed down a bottle of allergy pills with Jack Daniels. My nosy sister Sharla burst into the room I shared with my brothers Toby and Charlie and saw me lying in a puddle of vomit on the floor. Toby and Charlie were outside playing football with their friends. Anyway, the ambulance arrived and the paramedics did their job.

The second time was when I was eighteen and especially depressed because high school was over and I knew what was expected of me. I didn't want to be a sack boy at Piggly Wiggly or a waiter at Cracker Barrel. So I washed down a bottle of aspirin with Jim Beam. This time my mother discovered me in a puddle of vomit on the bathroom floor. Ambulance. Paramedics. On the psych ward a nurse said, "You again? Cat boy?" I said, "Yes. I see you're as dull and hygienically challenged as before." I was never voted Most Likely To Succeed on the psych ward, nor was I elected Mr. Congeniality.

The third time was last night. I snorted quite a lot of cocaine in Fuck City and guzzled seven or eight whiskey sours. I was more depressed than usual because I could not locate an acceptable fuck accomplice. Here I am. Business as usual on the psych ward. Suicide watch for the first twenty-four hours. They bring the food to me, which is nice.

I never write a letter. If I were to write a letter it would read like this:

Ysxubgfrc. Kvebuiuc. Phgizhigeeig.
Jchkhgiemxg. Ibhizhgiemr. Lcbijivee.
Iiiiiiiiiiiiiiiignujge. Hlcielkjice. Ixutong.
Quehziehipid. Yyyyviehgive. Bbbbb. Ztuigvc.
Yyyyyyyy. Yyyyyyyyyyy. Yyyyyyyyyyyyyy.
Five times five is twenty-five.
Brown is blue is yellow is orange is purple.
The Beatles The Rolling Stones Nirvana Dirt Dress.
Que. Que. Que. Que. Que. Que. Que. Que. Que. Que.

Wu-Tang Clan ain't nuttin' ta fuck wit.

Meow. Meow. Meow.
Meow. Meow. Meow.
Meow. Meow. Meow.

The world isn't interested in listening that hard.
And by listening I mean trying to decipher the gobbledygook
of a certified madman.

When I'm dead this will all make perfect sense.
Of that I am quite certain.

AMERICAN SOAP OPERA

It's an American soap opera created in 1971 by Rose Diana Wakefield, a Capricorn with Leo rising and a Pisces moon. The soap has been going strong for over three decades. The actors continue to win awards. The title is "Fast Forward To Tomorrow." The principal characters are:

Curtis Greenbriar…rich white patriarch
Emma Greenbriar…rich white matriarch
Elizabeth Greenbriar Mitchell…boring
Jane Greenbriar Walton…feisty
Thomas Greenbriar…narcissistic sociopath
Parker Mitchell…married to Elizabeth, fucking donut shop chick
Jacob Walton…married to Jane, fucking Elizabeth
Kaysi Cheddar…donut shop chick, infatuated with Thomas
Moondrop Paisley…wise eccentric astrologer

The soap is set in the fictional town of Sugar Valley, Texas. The action mostly takes place in the Greenbriar mansion and the donut shop.

It's Halloween and the annual Gleeful Pumpkin Ball is taking place at the Greenbriar mansion. All the rich fabulous immaculate motherfuckers are there, in costume.

Emma Greenbriar (dressed as Marie Antoinette): My dear, I am so glad you could come.

Kaysi Cheddar (dressed as a French maid): Thank you. I don't really know anyone here except for Parker and Thomas.

Emma Greenbriar: Of course. That is because you are fucking Parker and stalking Thomas.

Kaysi Cheddar: I…I didn't think you knew.

Emma Greenbriar: My darling girl, I know everything. I am a rich white matriarch, after all.

Kaysi Cheddar: Oh. Yeah. Of course. These hot wings are incredible.

Emma Greenbriar: But you aren't eating them.

Kaysi Cheddar: I don't eat anything. This is an American soap opera. I cannot speak with smeared lipstick and food stuck between my teeth.

Later. In one of the spotless minimally decorated (there are white and beige towels and a white and beige abstract painting…no toothbrushes) bathrooms.

Kaysi Cheddar: Thomas, I've been meaning to suck your dick for quite some time.

Thomas Greenbriar: Isn't Parker enough for you, Kaysi Cheddar?

Kaysi Cheddar: Obviously not. He fills the hours. But you're the one I think about when playing with my Hello Kitty vibrator. I crave you. I want you so bad I can already taste you. Thomas Greenbriar: I can't say I blame you. Okay, babe. Get to work. Slobber that knob.

Meanwhile. On the patio. Oh. Yeah. Thomas Greenbriar is dressed as a pimp, fro wig and all.

Elizabeth Greenbriar Mitchell (dressed as Paris Hilton): Parker. I just thought you should know that the maid saw Kaysi Cheddar go into the guest bathroom with Thomas. I'm certain they are having some kind of sex.
Parker Mitchell (dressed as a hotdog): That's cool.
Elizabeth Greenbriar Mitchell: I know you've been fucking Kaysi Cheddar for the past six months. There isn't anything cool about fucking a donut shop chick.
Parker Mitchell: It's just sex. Nothing else to do in this damn town. You know I don't care about football or backgammon or hunting or Jesus.
Elizabeth Greenbriar Mitchell: Once upon a time you enjoyed fucking me.
Parker Mitchell: Maybe it's just a phase I'm going through. I just see you as a vanilla ice cream cone and right now I'm craving rocky road.
Elizabeth Greenbriar Mitchell: Your road will be rocky indeed if you continue fucking a donut shop chick. You'll get her pregnant and there will be a boring scandal and I'll have to

divorce you and you'll lose everything and end up in a travel trailer next to a pawn shop. Is that what you want?
Parker Mitchell: Right now I want to smoke a bowl. Excuse me.

Moondrop Paisley, dressed as Elizabeth Taylor as Cleopatra, is sitting on the sofa in the media room watching a 1977 Italian porno with Jacob Walton. Jacob Walton is dressed as Colonel Sanders.

Jacob Walton: You know my situation, Moon. Help.

Moondrop Paisley: It's like I keep telling you, Jakey. Elizabeth will never satisfy you. She's a boring Capricorn with a boring Virgo ascendant and a boring Taurus moon. You and Jane aren't really compatible, either. She's much too exciting for you. All that Aries and Scorpio. You're just a basic ass Gemini. The girl for you is Kaysi Cheddar.
Jacob Walton: The donut shop chick? Nah. She's fucking Parker and Thomas. She's much too skanky for my blood.
Moondrop Paisley: She isn't skanky at all. Kaysi Cheddar is in fact your sensual soulmate.
Jacob Walton: My sensual soulmate? What the hell is that?
Moondrop Paisley: There is a damn near infinity of kinds of soulmates. Animal soulmates. You don't, or shouldn't, have sex with those. My cat Lester Bangs is my animal soulmate. I do not desire my cat in a sexual way. I simply feel better having

my cat around. Platonic soulmates. You and I are platonic soulmates. I do not find you sexually appealing but I can
say categorically that you are mildly attractive and pleasant
enough to exchange energy with on an occasional basis. I do
not crave your company but I enjoy it. Plutonic soulmates will
kill you if you let them. They inspire obsession and masoch-
ism. These kind of entanglements can result in self-harm,
maybe even suicide. Kaysi Cheddar is your sensual soulmate.
You could quite possibly achieve orgasm just by playing with
Kaysi Cheddar's hair.
Jacob Walton: Damn.
Moondrop Paisley: Your Libra moon is in Kaysi Cheddar's
fourth house. Kaysi's Aquarius sun is in your first house. To
be graphic, it's just a matter of time before your dick is in her
mouth.
Jacob Walton: Nah. I'm hung up on Elizabeth. Fuck astrology.
Elizabeth has the best tits I have ever experienced.

Curtis Greenbriar, dressed as God, is hanging out with his
favorite daughter in the kitchen. The walls are pale yellow.
The counters are white marble. The refrigerator is chrome.
Jane Greenbriar Walton is dressed as Vivien Leigh as Scarlett
O'Hara.

Curtis Greenbriar: You're the only person in the family who is
worth a damn.
Jane Greenbriar Walton: Daddy, you're sweet. But you're
drunk. Drunker than a skunk.

Curtis Greenbriar: You know…I've never understood that saying. Are skunks drunk? How are skunks any more inebriated than any other animal?

Jane Greenbriar Walton: Skunks don't drink alcohol unless they get into garbage that may contain bottles and cans with remnants of wine or beer or vodka or what the hell ever. The saying comes from skunks eating fermented fruits and berries which have fallen from trees and bushes. They become intoxicated from such. Also. Skunks are nocturnal creatures. They get drunk on the moon.

Curtis Greenbriar: See, my darling daughter. That is one of the many reasons why I love you so. You are the shining star of the family. I reiterate. You are the only person in the family who is worth a damn. Why you didn't go to Harvard Business School is beyond me. You could have if you had wanted to. And yes, precisely. I am drunk. Drunker than a damn skunk. I'm always drunk. There is nothing to be said for sobriety when you are seventy-six years old and stuck in Sugar Valley, Texas.

Jane Greenbriar Walton: But you love Mama. And you enjoy fishing and golfing and collecting rare first editions.

Curtis Greenbriar: I'll tell you the truth, darling girl. I never stopped loving Penelope Sanchez. I still dream of her often. I wonder what my life would have been like if I'd ignored my racist parents and said a big old FUCK YOU to the status quo and followed my damn heart.

Jane Greenbriar Walton: That kills me, Daddy. Oh my God. I am so so sorry.

Curtis Greenbriar: Ah, well. If I had married Penelope Sanchez there would be no you. And I am so so glad there is a you.

Jane Greenbriar Walton: I'm glad there's a me, too. But I would have been born, regardless. I would have just been born prettier and browner.

Curtis Greenbriar: We've got to find you a better husband. Jacob is a dud.

Jane Greenbriar Walton: Oh Jake will do, Daddy. We're going to the Bahamas in April. Shit gets solved in the Bahamas.

Curtis Greenbriar: Don't ever lose that fire, Janey.

Jane Greenbriar Walton: Don't worry, Daddy. It is well with my soul.

STRAWBERRY DOUCHE COMMERCIAL

Soap isn't enough, girlfriend. You've got to insert that plastic nozzle on a regular ass basis. During your period. After sex. After an invigorating vibrator session. Before sex. Treat your man or who the hell ever to some strawberry yogurt! You don't want to lose your boo thang to a donut shop chick, do you?

LAUNDRY DETERGENT COMMERCIAL

You have a life, maybe. You have to make it to the mall before traffic gets batshit. You have to get that gluten free lasagna in the oven before hubby gets home from the law firm. Goddamn Good & Clean laundry detergent does all the dirty work so you don't have to. Toss the clothes in the washer. One scoop is all it takes. Your darlings will bury their faces in the clean laundry and say, "Gee, Mom. You're magic."

Now it's the Monday following the Gleeful Pumpkin Ball. Kaysi Cheddar is walking to the donut shop from her apartment. A homeless guy in a Cookie Monster t-shirt approaches Kaysi Cheddar.

Homeless Guy: Hey baby doll. Can you spare a couple of bucks?

Kaysi Cheddar: Fuck off. I've got pepper spray.

Homeless Guy: Jesus loves you.

Kaysi Cheddar: Strive for singularity. That's the same tired shit people always say. Why doesn't anyone ever say Hitler loves you or Buddha loves you or Richard Ramirez loves you or Truman Capote loves you or Jerry Springer loves you or Abraham Lincoln loves you or Madonna loves you or Rick James loves you? Jesus gets entirely too much goddamn press.

Parker Mitchell appears. He's wearing a lime green golf shirt and dark green golf pants. His face is clean and angular. His eyes are flashing with anger at the perceived threat.

Parker Mitchell: Are you okay, babe? Is this asshole giving you shit?

Homeless Guy: I'm good, bro.

Parker Mitchell: I was talking to my friend. Get the hell out of here before I show you what an alpha male protecting his woman looks like.

Kaysi Cheddar: I'm fine, Parker. Why are you following me?

Parker Mitchell: We need to talk.

As Kaysi Cheddar performs her menial donut shop tasks Parker Mitchell pleads his case.

Parker Mitchell: Baby. I need you.

Kaysi Cheddar: You've got Elizabeth. Don't be greedy. Don't be a pig.

Parker Mitchell: I don't want Elizabeth. You're my sensual soulmate.

Kaysi Cheddar: Sensual soulmate? What the hell? What are you, suddenly? A Hindu? A crystal clutching New Age freak-tard?

Parker Mitchell: There you go again. Talking way over my head. I don't know what any of that means.

Kaysi Cheddar: Google is your BFF.

Parker Mitchell: Look, baby. All I know is that when I'm with Elizabeth I'm thinking of you. I can't get you out of my head. I try to lose myself in golfing. Doesn't work. It's you you you 24/7. It's like I've got this movie screen in my mind and all I see and hear is you. Your face and all the rest of you. You can't deny our bond. I don't know why you hooked up with Thomas at the party but he's nothing. He's scum. We have something real, something much deeper and more beautiful than booty quaking sex. You know we do, baby. Baby! Stop making the damn donuts and look at me! Please!

Kaysi Cheddar: I think I'm a nihilist, Parker. I enjoyed sucking Thomas off in the boring beige guest bathroom. I don't think of you whenever I'm not with you. I think of Thomas. He's an asshole. I dig his sociopathic energy. I'm awash in limerence. It's because my daddy took off with a Hungarian hooker when I was four. I'm not cut out for vanilla Five Below Bath & Body Works monogamy and the Olive Garden Cracker Barrel status quo.

Parker Mitchell: Congratulations, sweetheart. You just decimated me. I'm nothing now. I'm a dead cockroach. My guts are smeared all over the sole of your Payless shoe.

Thomas Greenbriar is in his office. He is looking out his window at the rising sun as he talks to some hot shit real estate agent on his hot shit iPhone.

Thomas Greenbriar: Yeah it has to be Calabasas. Malibu is trash. And the Mexican tile is non-negotiable. Call me back when you have something real to offer.

Laura is Thomas Greenbriar's preternaturally pretty and perky secretary. She looks and talks like Kelly Ripa. She also looks and talks like Reese Witherspoon. She also looks and talks like Cameron Diaz.

Laura: Mr. Greenbriar, you're all set for Cabo. Your flight leaves at seven tomorrow morning.
Thomas Greenbriar: Thanks, Laura. Are you feeling dangerous?
Laura: I can't go with you. You know that. I have to hold down the fort.
Thomas Greenbriar: Come on. You've earned a vacation.
Laura: You need a girlfriend, Mr. Greenbriar.
Thomas Greenbriar: I don't know about that.
Laura: What about Kaysi Cheddar?
Thomas Greenbriar: You must be joking. She's a donut shop chick.
Laura: I was at the ball. We all saw you go into the bathroom together.
Thomas Greenbriar: Shit. That was nada. Just a basic blow job. An efficient yet bloodless transaction.
Laura: So you want blood?
Thomas Greenbriar: Hell yeah I want blood. I'm a shark.

Elizabeth Greenbriar Mitchell is getting her hair done. While the dye seeps into her scalp she skims through the latest US

Weekly. Parker Mitchell walks into the salon.

Elizabeth Greenbriar Mitchell: Parker. What are you doing here?
Parker Mitchell: I'm going to kill you and then I'm going to kill myself.
Elizabeth Greenbriar Mitchell: Don't be an idiot. We're rich.
Parker Mitchell: Nothing matters. I'm a nihilist.

Parker Mitchell pulls out a gun of some kind, blows Elizabeth Greenbriar Mitchell's brains out and then puts the gun barrel in his mouth and pulls the trigger. This is an unusual American soap opera. You can see all the blood and gore. No trigger warning is provided.

Curtis Greenbriar speaks at the funeral. Everyone is dressed in black Armani and Christian Dior. The flowers are elegant and abundant. They are all white. The organ music is the usual banal bullshit.

Curtis Greenbriar: We all have blood on our hands. Not a one of us is exempt. Got some complicit motherfuckers up in this bitch. I always favored Jane. That's natural, of course. She's much more dynamic and charismatic and intelligent than her big sister could ever hope to be. I know Elizabeth sensed that I loved Jane more. Elizabeth couldn't help it that she was boring. She was cursed with a boring natal chart. Her mother always favored Thomas. Thomas the goddamn golden child. Thomas being Thomas, he never gave a hot damn about anyone but himself. He's in Cabo now with his secretary, Laura. She's a real shoo-in for Cameron Diaz. I'm sure they're having drunken sex on a white sand beach. Parker married Elizabeth for her money, naturally. He knew he'd never amount to dog shit on his own. Parker killed Elizabeth and himself over a blow job. The donut shop chick, Kaysi Cheddar, broke Parker's heart by telling him she enjoyed drinking Thomas's rich white cum during the Gleeful Pumpkin Ball. How do I know all of this sordid information? I'm the rich white patriarch. Basically, bitches…I am God. But unlike the real God who rained down hellfire on Sodom and Gomorrah I am far from perfect. There is no God, finally. We are all proof of that. Don't cry, babies. Don't smear that Maybelline. Look pristine for the goddamn cameras. A billion or so housewives are sitting on their fat asses living vicariously through all of us. We shall not disappoint.

American Racism 101

Take Beyonce. Take a lemonade stand. Take an elaborate social media campaign and a deep, thought provoking video. Take a perspicacious pugnacious team of writers. Take a fuckton of money. Take Taylor Swift. Take red lipstick. Make it Armani. Take diamonds. Lots and lots of diamonds. Take the fury of an unfucked skinny white woman. There's music beautiful motherfucking music to the madness. People in America dance to it Tweet to it twerk to it slurp to it sweat to it. Getting shit done since 1931. What happened in 1931? The Dust Bowl happened. Hell hath no fury like the Okie from Muskogee grapes of wrath. On May 1, 1931 the Empire State Building officially opened. Francis Scott Key Fitzgerald christened it with a bottle of Barnett & Fils Millesime Cognac Fine Champagne. He then proceeded to fuck Zelda Sayre Fitzgerald furiously in the elevator. She wept into her mink coat. This turned into a story. Also in 1931 Bela Lugosi thrilled and chilled in "Dracula." Warner Bros. released their first Merrie Melodies short: "Lady, Play Your Mandolin!" Unemployment (in America, where else) reached eight motherfucking million. In Texas one Reuben Crenshaw worked various ranches and competed in various rodeos. His sun was in Sagittarius. Nevada legalized all forms of gambling. Jupiter, which rules Sagittarius, also rules gambling and luck in general. "Little Orphan Annie" is transmitted like liquid gold on the goddamn American radio.

Clown Gravy

Take Uncle Remus. Take Tar-Baby. You fight goo. You get goo all over you. No one wins that bitch ass battle. Take Prissy. So black and small and silly. Don't know nothin' 'bout birthin' no babies. Take Scarlett. So white and mighty and determined. "As God is my witness, as God is my witness they're not going to lick me. I'm going to live through this and when it's all over, I'll never be hungry again. No, nor any of my folk. If I have to lie, steal, cheat or kill." Take Billie Holiday. Skip that lipstick. Take Patsy Cline. Why can't he be you? Take Ray Charles. I want you to hold my hand. Yeah, tight as you can. Take Frank Sinatra. Fill my heart with song. Let me sing forevermore. Take Tupac Shakur. First off fuck your bitch and the clique you claim. Take Marky Mark. Yeah. Can you feel it, baby? I can, too.

Take fried pies and potato salad and Mr. Pibb and white cream gravy and onion rings and Coca-Cola in green glass bottles and putting salty peanuts in the Coca-Cola in Seymour, Texas in 1977. Texas our Texas. All hail the mighty state. Don't look at the teenage pregnancies. Please don't pay attention to Uvalde, Texas. Please don't scrutinize May 24, 2022. Please don't take away our guns. Don't Google James Byrd Jr. dragging in Jasper, Texas. Don't remember The Alamo. Don't look at the CPS caseloads. Look away. Look away. Look away. Dixie Land.

Take tofu and kale and green tea and avocados and almonds and spinach smoothies and basic bitch SJW Facebook posts. Oh California. So vastly superior. California can teach Texas a thing or two or three about race relations in 21ˢᵗ Century America. San Francisco. Sanctuary City. Lowell High School. Who has time for statistics? You can dig deep enough and find anything. California rocks and all the hookers in the Tenderloin know it! The thing is…California is a kind of heaven. You have to die to go there.

Take anything in Arkansas. Take anything in West Virginia. Take $100 steaks (they massage the baby cows as soon as they're born…the baby moo cows are massaged all the way to the slaughterhouse) in Las Vegas. Take $100 cocktails in Calabasas. Oh Khloe. Girllll. You soooo loco. Take Frida Kahlo and her blood and her tortillas. Take Elizabeth Taylor and her diamonds and her drugs and her huge Pisces corazon (Richard Burton called her Ocean, among other things) and AIDS research and friendship with Michael Jackson. Is the jury still out on Jesus Juice? Ah. Fuck it. Don't stop 'til you get enough. "Off The Wall" covers a multitude of sins. Take Dick. Take Jane. See Dick run. Run, Dick. Run. See Jane smile. Smile, Jane. Smile. Take any motherfucking American primer. We got some learnin' to do. Back to the basics of love. Waylon Jennings can take us there but that means ya gotta put on a pair of faded jeans and cowboy boots and haul ass to Luckenbach. That's in Texas so good luck with that. Take Too Short. Lesson fo. Keep ya ho. It's the most important thing to know. O-Town. That's Oakland, y'all. Represent, yo. 510.

Then there's Louisiana. New Orleans. A white woman born in Bridgeport, Texas once asked a white man (when the man died the woman found out he was Jewish) born in Oakland, California of all the places he had ever lived (Oakland, San Francisco, New York City, Italy, Japan, Thailand, New Orleans) which place felt most like home. He didn't even have to think about it. "New Orleans," he said. Voodoo. Hoodoo. The white woman born in Bridgeport, Texas was told all her life that she had Cherokee ancestry on both sides. Then in 2018 or 2019 her little brother did the research at ancestry.com. No Cherokee but Creole on the mother's side. Creole ancestors buried in East Texas and Louisiana. Even before learning of the Creole ancestry the white woman was filling glass jars with magickal stuff and burying the magick jars in her white ex-husband's backyard. Candles. Sage. Incense. Cinnamon. Five finger grass. Bitch we will take all the help we can get. There's the bayou. There's Hank Williams making musical sense. Kinfolk come to see Yvonne by the dozen. Mardi Gras. Who will be crowned king? The suspense is killing me.

And I was like. And I was literally. And I was totally. Seriously. I can't even. Oh my actual god. For real though. Legit. Lit as fuck. Woke as fuck. Are we in the San Fernando Valley or are we in Appalachia or are we in the ghetto or are we in the barrio or are we in the trailer park or are we on a reality television show updating our Facebook status (it's like literally complicated) while we get our toenails painted? I will fuck you up. Trust. I went there. Literally. You ain't shit, dawg. I can't even. Oh my god. Literally. McFUCK.

Say Sally has to make it to Denver from San Antonio before Brad decides he'd rather Netflix and chill with Monique. Sally has negative sixty dollars in her checking account. Sally lost her T-Mobile phone due to nonpayment. Tommy Lee has a really big dick and bitch, it's pierced. Kanye West retweeted my latest selfie. I'm Google rich and PayPal poor. Pero. Sally needs to lose twenty-three pounds. Sally's brain is a slice of watermelon populated with happy ants. Sally isn't black. Sally is white. This is how we identify motherfuckers in the U.S.A. today. The asshole wasting time and energy in the Ovaltine Office is a talking Cheeto. He's going to MAGA. Great Value condoms. Great Value grape jelly. Great Value Vaseline. Great Value gluten-free Pop-Tarts. MAGA. MAGA. One of us. If you aren't Gen X you won't get the reference. "Freaks." 1932. Gooble. Gobble. We accept her. We accept her. One of us. One of us. The Ramones were sufficiently impressed. Sally doesn't have any credit cards. Sally needs a blow job. Sally has a vagina. Vaginas don't get blow jobs. Sally fantasizes sometimes that she has a dick and she's fucking herself. Sally identifies as Sexually Vanilla With A Dark Chocolate Swirl. Sally has never fucked anyone other than Cougar but Sally fantasizes about Diablo. Diablo is in some kind of gang. Looks tough as shit in his blue bandana. This is for La Raza.

There are plenty of other American examples. Ashton Kutcher is irrelevant to many yet motherfucker can move to Fiji tomorrow if he so desires. Cameron Diaz? Yeah. Same thing. Audrey Hepburn. Marilyn Monroe. Facebook freak-tards continue to wish Marilyn Monroe HAPPY BIRTHDAY and quote the icon because she was like really deep and philosophical and so tragic. May the Kennedy brothers burn in HELL! Marlon Brando. Blah yada blah. James Dean. Archie. Betty. Veronica. Fat Albert. Pink Panther. Strawberry Shortcake. Shit gets DONE in America. My Little Pony? Hello Kitty? Uh. Yeah. Like. Totally. Buy a new bra. Make damn sure it's cleavage enhancing. Buy a new dildo. No. Buy more than one. Buy every damn color of the rainbow. Fuck yourself with the black dildo on Monday. Fuck yourself with the white dildo on Tuesday. Fuck yourself with the brown dildo on Wednesday. Black and white and brown are not featured in the rainbow. Purple. Green. Red. Go on go on with your bad rainbow ass self. I identify as cerulean. White is not a race. White is the most useless Crayola. White is the most boring wall. Bring on the graffiti.

Someday you won't be able to tell what anyone is. In 2047 or 2059 maybe you won't be able to look at someone and say, "Yep. There goes another white/black/brown bitch. Must be nice."

"What will we do when everyone kind of just blends in? How will we identify when there are no more races?" the beige woman asks the beige man.

"Humans will always find something to create division. The monsters own Maple Street," the beige man replies. They both live for the Fourth of July "Twilight Zone" marathons.

The older I get the more I want to send every motherfucker to the cornfield.

White blah and white yada and beige redundancy and Google it I swear to GOD no joke it's a thing. I love fried chicken. I hate watermelon. I love Too Short. I hate Toby Keith. My Latino ex called me "hillbilly." I can scrub and scrub with Warm Vanilla Sugar body wash but alas. Alas. I remain a basic bitch from the North Texas sticks.

Cougar is whiter than his Fruit of the Looms. Cougar was happy to see Obama exit and Trump enter. Cougar uses the "N" word but only around his bowling buddies.

"Can't trust a motherfucker. Motherfuckin' pussy ass special snowflake bitch gonna run to Facebook Twitter Instagram YouTube WordPress police. Mommy! Daddy! Make Cougar stop hatin'!"

"We do not inhabit a snowglobe world."

"Huh?"

"Don't play dumb, Cougar. You know exactly what the fuck I'm talkin' about, Willis. A snowglobe. You've owned at least one in your privileged life. It's plastic. You shake it. Maybe there's a red and white Santa Claus inside. Snow that isn't really snow swirls around. People think it's the world we actually live in. Like the world we actually live in is that small and pretty and plastic and kitschy and contained. The background is definitely bright blue. Ain't no mistakin' that color. It's pretty fuckin' blatant. Santa's bag and boots are always black. The reindeer that guide Santa's sleigh are always brown. What else could Frosty be but white? Snow is white. Frosty is a snowman…or snow person…made from snow. I didn't write the rules. I guess Frosty could be yellow, theoretically, if the reindeer or elves or Santa pissed in the snow. That is not a racial slur. I am not comparing Asians to piss. Asians aren't really yellow, are they? Big Bird is definitely yellow. Got my street smarts from PBS. Anyway. Piss is various shades of yellow. Can be brownish. Can be golden. Sometimes piss is red and that's when you know you got more than 99 problemas. But yeah. The snowglobe is cute on a shelf with Hula Doll and Fritz The Cat and Luke Skywalker and Confederate flag shot glass and ironic Jesus candle and Kurt Cobain action figure and Disability Barbie. Wheelchair not included. You know exactly what the fuck is up."

"Ain't nothin' ironic about Jesus, boy. He's my personal Lord and Savior. He died for your sins and mine and every damn body's and don't you fuckin' forget that shit."

"Did Jesus die for Kanye West and Angela Davis and Beyonce and Blac Chyna and Obama and Muhammad Ali and Malcolm X and Richard Pryor and Fats Domino and Samuel L. Jackson and Michael Jackson and Janet Jackson and Oprah and Whoopi and Dr. Dre?"

"Jesus definitely died for Beyonce. Hell. I'd die for that fine ass bitch any day of the week."

"Of course you would. But Cougar. I am being serious. Serious as a fucking heart attack. You believe Jesus was correct to die for you and Thomas Jefferson and Thomas Edison and Ava Gardner and Shirley Temple and Stephen King and Jim Henson and Babe Ruth and Tom Hanks and Julia Roberts and Dolly Parton and Burt Reynolds and Miley Cyrus. No error there. Jesus can't wait to see your white ass walk through the pearly gates. Correct, Cougar?"

"Look. Dude. I didn't ask to be born white like Jesus. It just happened that way. Did I ask to be born to Wayne and Judy Ketchup? No. Did I ask to be born in Fort Worth, Texas? No. I did not. My birth was an accident. I didn't sign up for any of this. Am I glad to be a white Texan American? You bet your sweet ass I am. I thank God for the accident that is me."

"Jesus wasn't white."

"Well. Now you're just being a politically correct pawn but that's cool, dude. Someone's gotta swig the Kool-Aid. All I know is what I learned in Sunday school. Jesus was the original redneck. He hung out with some cool ass motherfuckers. And in all the pictures you can clearly see he has pale skin, light brown hair and blue eyes. And I guarandamntee ya if Jesus could've chosen to be born in Texas he'd have been all over that shit."

"Why Texas?"

"Now you're just bein' an idiot on purpose. Who the hell wants to be born in Egypt or Italy or Mexico or Ohio or New Jersey or Rhode Island? One thing about Texans. We know who the fuck we are. We ain't confused. I know I got a big white dick. I know I love me some pink pussy. I know Reagan was the best damn president ever but Trump is a close second. I know I like my beer cold and my steak hot and bloody. I love blow jobs, coconut pie, Dallas Cowboys and the Texas flag. I sleep just fine at night and dream of big white titties."

Take a nap. Take a break. Take a breath. Are you making the world brighter and better than ever before with your tweets and pictures of your big deal brunch and brand-new kitten? Is your beige redundancy the best thing ever stuck inside a Crayola box? Does it matter? Any of it? Your histrionics? Your manufactured outrage? Your blog vomit manifesto?

Take Tarantino. Take John Travolta. Take the boxing match on Saturday. Take Brooklyn. Take Houston. Take French fries. Take tater tots. Take Otis Redding. Take "Pretty in Pink." Take Blondie. Take MTV. Take your mama. Take a number. Take it all off. Crayolas gone wild.

PRETTY RED BERRIES

A few years before Merissa met Andres in San Antonio she had a dream so vivid that she turned it into a poem of several pages and published it herself. When she had the dream Merissa was living with her second husband and their infant son in what she called the crack whore shack in Nederland, Texas. Merissa needed and needed and needed and did not have. She tried to dance the small press disco at MySpace and failed miserably. So many options. Unhappily married editors and poets. Let's play patty cake patty cake baker's man. All around the goddamn mulberry bush. No. This ain't it. How many selfies does it take? A bitch tries with fried hair and Wet N Wild makeup and fishnets. A bitch finally folds.

In the dream Merissa was in an enormous warehouse with hundreds of illegal immigrants. They were being herded like cattle to their execution. When Merissa's name was finally called the aluminum door rolled up and she was standing on a dock facing Texas Border Patrol. They pointed their machine guns at Merissa and asked her if she wanted to consult the priest and if she had any last words. Merissa discovered that she was standing in front of a holly bush.

"Fuck the priest. I ain't Catholic," Merissa said. She spread her arms and said, "Make pretty red berries." The bullets flew and Merissa's blood splattered the glossy green leaves. Then she was flying over the Rio Grande, looking down at Mexicans swimming across to Texas where they could sweat their asses off for five bucks an hour and get fat on dollar store soda and Little Debbie snack cakes. Then Merissa was flying over a parking lot. A tired woman was pushing her shopping cart toward her SUV. "Thank God I'm done with the clatter," Merissa said. She flew higher and higher until she melted.

Misti Rainwater-Lites shuffles cards wearing fake fingernails and Party City wigs for a living. She writes books and creates art and sings karaoke to get through this thing called life in San Antonio, Texas.

MORE ROADSIDE PRESS TITLES:

By Plane, Train or Coincidence
Michele McDannold

Prying
Jack Micheline, Charles Bukowski and Catfish McDaris

Wolf Whistles Behind the Dumpster
Dan Provost

Busking Blues: Recollections of a Chicago Street Musician and Squatter
Westley Heine

Unknowable Things
Kerry Trautman

How to Play House
Heather Dorn

Kiss the Heathens
Ryan Quinn Flanagan

St. James Infirmary
Steven Meloan

Street Corner Spirits
Westley Heine

A Room Above a Convenience Store
William Taylor Jr.

Resurrection Song
George Wallace

MORE ROADSIDE PRESS TITLES:

Nothing and Too Much to Talk About
Nancy Patrice Davenport

Bar Guide for the Seriously Deranged
Alan Catlin

Born on Good Friday
Nathan Graziano

Under Normal Conditions
Karl Koweski

The Dead and the Desperate
Dan Denton